Daniel

DANIEL

Under the Siege of the Divine

Daniel Berrigan

The Plough Publishing House

Acknowledgments
Scripture quotations from the *New Revised Standard Version of the Bible* © 1989 by the Division of Christian Education of the National Council of Churches of Christ in the USA. Used with permission.
"Vocabulary," from *Last Waltz in Santiago,* by Ariel Dorfman. Copyright © 1988 by Ariel Dorfman and Edith Grossman. Used by permission of Viking Penguin, a division of Penguin Putnam Inc.
"Not Even Mythology" is reprinted from Yannis Ritsos, *Repetitions Testimonies Parentheses.* Copyright © 1991 by Princeton University Press. Reprinted by permission of Princeton University Press.
The excerpt from "From A German War Primer" is reprinted from Bertolt Brecht, *Poems 1913–1956,* © 1976 by Eyre Methuen, Inc. Used with permission.
"A Mirror for the Twentieth Century" is reprinted from Abdullah Al-Udhari, ed., *Modern Poetry of the Arab World,* © 1986 by Penguin Books Ltd. Used with permission.
"On the Threshold of Tomorrow" is reprinted from Vahan Tekeyan, *Sacred Wrath: Selected Poems of Vahan Tekeyan* (Ashod Press, 1982), © 1982 by Diana Der Hovanessian. Used with permission.
Excerpt from *The Cure at Troy: A Version of Sophocles' Philoctetes* by Seamus Heaney. Copyright © 1990 by Seamus Heaney. Reprinted by permission of Farrar Straus and Giroux, Inc.
"Looking at Stars" copyright 1996 Jane Kenyon. Reprinted from *Otherwise: New and Selected Poems* with the permission of Graywolf Press, Saint Paul, Minnesota.

A catalog record for this book is available from the British Library.

Library of Congress Cataloging-in-Publication Data

Berrigan, Daniel
Daniel, under the siege of the Divine / Daniel Berrigan.
p. cm.
ISBN 0-87486-952-8
1. Bible. O. T. Daniel--Commentaries. I. Bible. O. T. Daniel. English. New Revised Standard. 1998. II. Title.
BS1555.3.B45 1998
224'.5077--dc21 98-14517
CIP

Printed in the USA

Contents

Introit
Under the Siege of the Divine

We speak of faith, and we are accustomed to ask: what has this fey, transcendental, religious thing to do with the hustle and bustle, the burn and iron of life? But it is there, as large and as hard as the everyday life of nations and human society.

In faith there is a need of a unique combination of sentiments and ideas, faith and questioning, seriousness and irony, illusion and reality. I call it the body of the sensibility of faith. It has taken several thousands of years to shape this sensibility for what it is – a complex, highly developed instrument for the handling of many things, birth, life, death, and faith itself. Faith, therefore, is not an isolated thing, limited to some secret place in the soul.

William Lynch, S.J.

Vocabulary

Show me a word I can use.
Show me one verb.
An adjective as clear as a ray of light.
Listen carefully to the bottom of every sentence,
to the attic and the dust in the furniture
of every sentence,

perk up your ears,
Listen and look under the bed
of every sentence
at the soldier waiting their turn
at the foot
of the bride's bed.

To preserve just one word.
What is it to be?

Like a question on a quiz show.
If you could take one word with you
to the future,
what is it to be?

Find it.
Plunge into the garbage heap.
Stick your hands deep into the ooze.
Close your fist around the fragment of a mirror
fractured by feet that dance on what should have been
a wedding night.

Let me tell you something.
Even if I had been there
I could not have told their story.

I was calling from another country
and the phone was still busy.
I was trying to call home
and the machine had just swallowed
my last dime.

As for the story I cannot tell.
They accumulated tenderness
as others accumulated money.
Ask them.
Even if the phone is busy.
Even if the machine has just swallowed your last dime.

Even if the operator drowns out all the other voices.
Ask them for the verse our lovers will still need
if we ever again to bathe
in the same river.

Let them speak for themselves.

Ariel Dorfman

The consummate artistry of this book! And yet, strange to our eyes, the artist Daniel is not included in the Hebrew bible as a prophet. His book finds place there under a heading known as "Writings," together with such versatilities as Psalms, Job, The Song of Songs, Ecclesiastes, Proverbs, and so on. Is the book then to be thought essentially unclassifiable? What do Jews make of Daniel? Ambiguity is the note in the Talmud. Yes, he is a prophet; no, he is not. Only Ezekiel has met with a colder official glance.

And yet, and yet. From the sixth century BCE, the era of events recounted here, to the second, the era of final redaction, one senses the mighty leap of midrash.* For Christians there is an open door and a firm embrace. The book makes sense, divine and human, in whatever time. The heroic example of Daniel and his community offers a perennial blessing. Centuries after his lifetime, in an equally awful era, he speaks up, strong and clear, on behalf of the victims of our lifetime.

Is Daniel a prophet? One can, at the least, claim that his example, if not his intuitions, merit the laurel. That faith of Daniel! A faith, to borrow from William Lynch, "as large and as hard as the everyday life of nations and human society...a complex, highly developed instrument for the handling of...life, death, and faith itself." Daniel stood eye to eye with the powers, and survived. And what courage his survival exacted!

A further contention underlies the present commentary. Daniel's story continues today, verified again and again in events both awful and hopeful. The book is premonitory of the methods of tyrants, whether ancient or modern; better still, it is a salubrious story that offers strong relief and

*Midrash – a Talmudic explanation of the underlying significance of a biblical text.

insight. There are the principalities of today to be confronted, their idols and thrice-stoked furnaces and caves of lions, their absurd self-serving images and rhetoric. Someone must pink their pride, decode the handwriting on the wall! Who is to stand up, to withstand? Daniel and his like.

The ancient story tells of conflicts of conscience in opposition to the sordid will of the powers. And a like vocation continues for people of faith; in every age, they (we) must walk a thin line, a line drawn through a world quite as mad as that of Daniel and his all but unpronounceable adversaries. The line separates; it also joins and unites.

As to questions and themes undertaken in our book: shall the world claim us for its own? Or shall we claim one another in God's name, renouncing the world's tactics – murder, hatred, and injustice? The story concerns the wiles of worldly power, striking hard against the discipline of the believing community. In struggle, the faith of Daniel and his friends is revealed ironically as a new form of power. The book is also strangely concerned with dreams. The dreams are opaque to the powerful dreamers; only Daniel has access to their meaning.

To Daniel the dreams lay open matters which the powerful would much prefer to keep under wraps, concealed even from their own soul. The substance of the dreams? The obsession of the mighty with matters of control and domination, over people and property. An obsession that insults and exceeds nature, brings ruin to many, and eventually destroys the intemperate dreamers.

In decoding the dreams, Daniel unmasks the realm of the principalities, those spirits of vengeance, cruelty, lust, and greed. Thus by implication the book reveals the void, the emptiness that lies behind the fearsome brows of the powerful.

The book concerns obedience also: to torah, vows, covenant. The heavy cost of this, and its reward – the blessing that inevitably follows on fidelity. (As well as the opposite: radical disobedience, pride, thirst for power.)

Judgment is a theme. And the mighty condemn it, even as they undergo its rigors in nightmares of fear and dread. The lowly, on the contrary, hail its onset with joy; come liberation, come vindication!

There are also images of obsession and vain longing. The obsessed, it is shown, lord it over the grandiloquent (finally ridiculous) eminences who welcome such images. Images of royal ego abound; its vapidity and inflation. And in holy contrast, images of truth telling, truthful living.

The book calls us strongly in the direction of tradition; it would make of us a species of scriptural atavists. Every generation must learn from its remote ancestors the truths that evade the nearer ones. (There is a vexing question here for Catholics: where the connection, where the discontinuity between the teaching of current authority, and the noble founders and evangelists and martyrs of our tradition?) We are well advised to hearken with all our hearts' attention to our great-great ancestors like Daniel.

As Daniel demonstrates, there is obedience and obedience. One form tends to servility and shallowness; it hides out in the shadow of him-who-has-the-last-word. Over such conduct no cloud of witnesses hovers, no ancient ancestry, no text (or the text at hand is neglected, closed) no whispers and dreams beckoning. Servile obedience is like a clamorous parental voice at our ear, spelling out details, moral precepts, footnotes, jots and tittles. The law, always the law!

Drowned out is the ancestral hum and murmur, like a shell whispering of seven seas, vast horizons, long vistas of time. Calling us to one another, calling us home.

Taming the Beasts and the King of the Beasts

The Book of Daniel

I In the third year of the reign of King Jehoiakim of Judah, King
Nebuchadnezzar of Babylon came to Jerusalem and besieged it.
[2]The Lord let King Jehoiakim of Judah fall into his power, as well
as some of the vessels of the house of God. These he brought to the
land of Shinar, and placed the vessels in the treasury of his gods.

[3]Then the king commanded his palace master Ashpenaz to bring
some of the Israelites of the royal family and of the nobility, [4]young
men without physical defect and handsome, versed in every branch
of wisdom, endowed with knowledge and insight, and competent
to serve in the king's palace; they were to be taught the literature
and language of the Chaldeans. [5]The king assigned them a daily
portion of the royal rations of food and wine. They were to be educated for three years, so that at the end of that time they could be
stationed in the king's court. [6]Among them were Daniel, Hananiah, Mishael, and Azariah, from the tribe of Judah. [7]The palace
master gave them other names: Daniel he called Belteshazzar, Hananiah he called Shadrach, Mishael he called Meshach, and
Azariah he called Abednego.

[8]But Daniel resolved that he would not defile himself with the
royal rations of food and wine; so he asked the palace master to
allow him not to defile himself. [9]Now God allowed Daniel to receive favor and compassion from the palace master. [10]The palace
master said to Daniel, "I am afraid of my lord the king; he has
appointed your food and your drink. If he should see you in poorer
condition than the other young men of your own age, you would
endanger my head with the king." [11]Then Daniel asked the guard
whom the palace master had appointed over Daniel, Hananiah,
Mishael, and Azariah: [12]"Please test your servants for ten days. Let
us be given vegetables to eat and water to drink. [13]You can then
compare our appearance with the appearance of the young men
who eat the royal rations, and deal with your servants according to
what you observe." [14]So he agreed to this proposal and tested them
for ten days. [15]At the end of ten days it was observed that they

appeared better and fatter than all the young men who had been eating the royal rations. [16]So the guard continued to withdraw their royal rations and the wine they were to drink, and gave them vegetables. [17]To these four young men God gave knowledge and skill in every aspect of literature and wisdom; Daniel also had insight into all visions and dreams.

[18]At the end of the time that the king had set for them to be brought in, the palace master brought them into the presence of Nebuchadnezzar, [19]and the king spoke with them. And among them all, no one was found to compare with Daniel, Hananiah, Mishael, and Azariah; therefore they were stationed in the king's court. [20]In every matter of wisdom and understanding concerning which the king inquired of them, he found them ten times better than all the magicians and enchanters in his whole kingdom. [21]And Daniel continued there until the first year of King Cyrus.

Taming the Beasts and the King of the Beasts

Daniel 1:1–2 A despondent note opens the book. The worst of times is at hand, and no relief in sight. The holy city has fallen to pagans. More: the tragedy is attributed to the decree of God. A bitter pill indeed. God's will, the utter downfall of the chosen? An inevitable "yes" is the response of the prophets.

Those unambiguous, robust, fearless voices! Nowhere else, in no other culture, ancient or modern, is so devastating a critique launched on a people by their own. For this time, though, Daniel is far from unique in leveling his stupendous judgment. Jeremiah named the sacking of Jerusalem a judgment against the sins of his people (Jer. 21:1–7; 25:8–14). There is also Ezekiel, chapters 2, 4, and 6. And Lamentations is a long ululation for the deportation of the people of covenant, cowering under God's decree.

In 586 BCE, Jerusalem fell, its walls and temple ground to a rubble. Judaeans joined their exiled compatriots in Babylon. No temple could be built on foreign soil; no sacrifices could be offered, no pilgrimages undertaken. It is the end of a world; the proud Jerusalemites are reduced to branded slaves, frozen in time and place.

Under such catastrophe, existence itself is shaken. A tormented question arose: where was Jahweh, where the Shekinah,* of what help the Torah and the holy Ark? It was an unparalleled cultural disaster, equaled only by the Holocaust of our lifetime.

*Shekinah – the divine presence of God within the world.

This was a capital point, a poignard aimed at the heart. The God of Israel, some said in despair, had been bested by the god Marduk. Temple artifacts were rifled, transported by heathen hands, deposited blasphemously in the treasury of Nebuchadnezzar's god. Thenceforth, could the God of the Jews be worshipped, in whatever inadequate, sorrowful way, as true God?

Of our protagonist Daniel no ancestry is noted. He simply appears on the scene, a kind of Melchizedek. We know only that he has undergone the exile along with his compatriots. Unlike many, he has survived. Thus do the great appear in our midst – epiphanies, isolates, gifts of God. They surpass whatever promise the bloodline offers; nothing of genetics or circumstance explains their appearance, a near miracle.

We must account Daniel also a survivor, an artful dodger of the slings and arrows of a distempered time. An improviser of ways and means. An icon for the people of his lifetime, and for those to come, an heroic image of fidelity. All of these; and a high mystic as well.

In the Christian tradition he is honored as one of the sublime quaternity of the major prophets. In a window of the Cathedral of Chartres, an astonishing image glows: Daniel and his other "major" compatriots – Isaiah, Jeremiah, and Ezekiel – bear upon their shoulders the four evangelists.

Daniel 1:3–7 To begin our story, Daniel and three companions are chosen from among the exiles by the king. A distinction is thus conferred, with many a gratuity to follow! And a danger as well.

The tactic is common enough, and within the imperial ideology it makes sound sense. To wit; single out, segregate the best of an enslaved population. The irony starts here, and the danger as well. And the sowing of envy and confusion among the exiles.

As to the lucky few, the royal tactic emerges. Stroke their ego; offer compensations and comforts. Bond with them; enlist them in the adventure of empire. Offer relief from the rigors of exile; beckon them to the "good life." Thus a new, silken enslavement replaces the former brutal one. *Noblesse oblige.* Let the favored ones forget their compatriots in travail. Let the images and memories of suffering fade away. Let their former companions be reduced – to strangers, faceless "others."

The rewards accruing to the king's choice are apparent: access to the powerful, together with a carefully meted authority of one's own, prestige, citizenship in the high culture of empire. Never stated is the price to be exacted.

Daniel had been named, whether by parents consciously prophetic or not, "God is my judge." A name is thus attached to a life. And in time, it becomes clear that the life moves in consonance with the name. But now, a new name is conferred by the king. It is a first step toward assimilation; change the names of those (ironically) "chosen" anew, this time for Babylonian honors and riches.

Daniel is no longer Daniel. And the new name denotes neither Jahweh nor judgment. His name is now Belteshazzar: "O Bel, protect the king." Thus fealty is indicated. Let everyone who hears or pronounces the name realize that the (former) Daniel is liberated from former sovereignties; he is in service to a far different world vision.

And despite the overlay of exemptions and so on, let all know that Belteshazzar is now the king's close chattel. A new status? Not so new after all. It comes to this; nothing essential to his former life is altered. Like the slaves and exiles, he remains the property of the Babylonian tyrant.

The tactic is devilishly clever. Change the name, alter in superficial respects the fortunes. In the king's intent, the naming implies apostasy, alienation from a saving tradition, amnesia of soul; these and loss of community, of torah and prophets, of the memory of the saving deeds of God. The purpose is pure horror.

Communal memories are dangerous; they are joined to self understanding, even purpose of resistance. To own one's memories is to deny the imperial definition and decree: you are slaves. We are not slaves; we own our past, and affirm it daily, secretly; free. Dangerous. Such images must be weakened, then obliterated; they are the seedbed of hope. They are an outcry from the depths of the communal psyche. God, save your afflicted people!

But Daniel and his companions (so goes the imperial logic), these fortunate few, are already drawn forth; what need then of an outcry?

No greater honor; the "chosen" are to sit at the king's table. But there is a drawback, an obstacle. It is simple and definitive, and the youths know it. They cannot observe torah and still partake of the royal menu.

Daniel 1:8–16 They must therefore choose. We take note of the subtle effort to obscure all such choices. Why, what of simple gratitude? Has not the king himself singled them out? Shall that not suffice, and more? And shall they, so auspiciously chosen, choose now to make of a small matter a great?

We take note, and are edified. That Daniel's community see a choice looming, albeit a choice dangerous and difficult, is a precious evidence; their freedom is intact. They speak up.

It is a simple "no." They will abstain from the elegant meats of the palace table. On this small pivot all that is to follow, events whether serendipitous or tragic, turn.

And our story is underway. Two results of fidelity to torah are immediately apparent. The first may be ascribed to the natural benefits of abstinence: the youths' physical condition blooms and flourishes. But this is hardly the point of the story. The benefits, clear and glowing on the bodies of the resisters, are the sign of God's interior action. They flourish also in spirit. In reward for their difficult act of obedience, Jahweh confers on them a surpassing wisdom. Against it, all the machinations of the empire will batter in vain. The "system" that surrounds them, smiles on them – and would own them – is declared null and void.

Marked as they are for a distinction (of sorts), a temptation is inferred, obscure and menacing: "Come now, all this do I offer you, if you but fall down and adore…"

The primal force of their simple "no" is not easy to grasp. It is uttered by a few; they are strangers and aliens in a land of no mercy. In a sense that could only be called grievous, the youths are on their own. Little help is at hand to reinforce their faith; no temple liturgies, no synagogue, no rhythms of season or days to unroll the scripture afresh, and no elders to consult. (Were the sacred books accessible to exiles in a pagan court? We are told nothing.) The three must undergo a kind of forced growth induced by memory, that dangerous gift. This is their help, and it prevails. Conscience is infused mightily with the memory of torah. They know whence they come.

As tyrants beget tyrants, prophets and martyrs beget their like. Whatever their carnal ancestry, whatever their status among believers of the future, it is clear that Daniel and his friends are infused and animated by the prophets of their people. The inference is clear; their choice is grievously dangerous. Beyond doubt they are torn. Survival is a large issue. So is protection of one another, and the enfolding of a lorn people in the protection and power a few have attained. They stand at the threshold of influence, as they well know. But above all, they would be faithful.

The king's food, for reasons unexplained, is regarded as a defilement. Had the viands been offered to the gods? In any case, these favored ones are urged to become complaisant consumers. All benefits will follow. But they will not partake. Yielding to the king would be received by their people, as they well know, as an act of apostasy.

We pause over that sturdy "no." At this point of the story, it is Daniel's only word, his only offering, to the exiles, to the future. To ourselves. A gesture of grace, a simple monosyllable! On the lips of the resisters it becomes a word of worship; sorry and small to be sure, lonely, accompanied by no grandezza, no trumpets, promising no favorable outcome. A risky word on the tongue. His "no" is all Daniel can offer – and there is no altar to offer it on.

We hear that word, that refusal. We hear it repeated, echoed down the centuries, perhaps never more strongly than in our own day. We know, or know of, those who dare utter it. And of some who die for the utterance. A puny monosyllable; no sooner spoken, it seems lost on the air. And yet the word, like "a cloud no larger than a hand covers the sun."

Daniel's "no" shakes the thrones and the enthroned where they sit. (And one thinks of Bonhoeffer's "no," and that of Franz Jägerstätter, of the students of the White Rose, of Nelson Mandela, of Oscar Romero. And, as I set down these notes, the "no" of my brother Philip, of James and Gregory, of Susan and Stephen and Helen and Carl and Mark and

Tom,* of peacemakers far and near, some awaiting trial, others already convicted and imprisoned. And across the world, how many thousands, unknown, swell that sublime chorus!)

And then, of course, a different drummer, a different choice. The pinch of incense, the meat and wine of kings, the perks, the bowing of the knee. The taxes duly handed over, the draft registration, the military induction. The research and deployment and guarding of obscene weaponry, the paycheck...The crime of silence, of complicity.

We conjure, too, the setting in which Daniel's "no" was uttered; the sordid grandeur of the court, the prospering, the busy brokering and bargaining, the inflated egos, the void, the heartless heart of the empire. The atmosphere of secure power, the diplomatic but military give-and-take bruited about, the economic shifts and ploys, the diplomacy, the next move against the next enemy...It all comes to this: we, the titans, decide who shall prosper and who go under, who shall live and who die.

Then an interruption, a "no." The small secret start of something else. Someone, some few, move quietly out of lockstep. And the solid throne is ever so slightly jarred. The hideous dovetailing of violence and worldly prosperity; the cunning, the power arrogated, taken for granted, a metaphysical verity – all this suddenly is placed in question.

Daniel will make a large thing of this refusal, but only in his heart. In public, at least for a time, it were best to make it

*The people mentioned here all participated in what has become known as the 1997 Prince of Peace Plowshares action. Led by Philip Berrigan, the Plowshares group entered the Bath (Maine) Ironworks on Ash Wednesday to protest the production of guided missile destroyers. Subsequently arrested and tried, most of them are now serving prison terms.

a small thing, not to unnecessarily chafe "good order." For survival is also at stake. It is a lesser good compared to the greater. But it is also good, very good indeed, though (it must be said to one's own soul, as a koan* of sorts) "it is lesser, that good." And again and again, a voice speaks from the heart of reality: remember the first Good.

Daniel reminds us of other heroes: of St. Thomas More, perhaps, in a general way. Of those few who have served the powerful *in situ,* determined to keep to a rigorous moral order – a first, irreplaceable good, and a secondary, hypothetical one. First fidelity, then survival. Such are few, so few as to constitute a race apart. We call them saints. Many of them are martyrs.

A caveat, then, crucial to our understanding of the story of Daniel: he survives, even prospers. But it is hardly a success story. By no means are we to conclude that his steadfastness, his besting of the king and counselors, is a formula for prevailing over the powers that be.

The biblical word is austere; it sticks in the throat. Far different stories abound in its pages – stories of defeat and martyrdom; the books of Job, of Jeremiah, Isaiah, Habakkuk, the gospel of Jesus – these offer other, ominous outcomes. The principalities win out; they destroy the holy ones. Thus the Bible places us squarely at a wall; the stark, opaque, seemingly implacable irony we name Providence. Daniel is the exception. For a while. We learn much, and infer more. And we are appalled. God so often abandons his own to torture and execution. We think, in our day, of the multitudes of

*Koan – a paradox used by Zen teachers to encourage dependence not on reason or rational explanations, but on enlightenment.

disappeared and slaughtered in Chiapas, El Salvador, Guatemala, Nicaragua; of the children of Iraq, bombed and starving under wicked "sanctions," of those gunned down in the streets of Sarajevo and Kosovo; of hideous chambers of interrogation, of prisons and death rows across the world. Such deaths as occur daily! They testify to the cost of that "no" spoken by Daniel, a scripture verified in our bloodshot lifetime, "for our instruction."

Not Even Mythology

The day ends that way, with brilliant colors, so lovely, without
anything at all happening for us. The Guards forgotten in the
guardhouse…
And later, when the lamps were lit,
we went inside and again returned to Mythology, searching
for some deeper correlation, some distant, general allegory
to soothe the narrowness of the personal void. We found nothing.
The pomegranate seeds and Persephone seemed cheap to us
in view of the night approaching heavily and the total absence.

Yannis Ritsos

Thus we keep in sensible focus the story of Daniel, together with its fortunate and altogether rare ending. Daniel's is a story of providence, not of success. A story of obedience, its risks and rewards. In a later episode, Daniel's life is placed in jeopardy; he hangs by a thread above the brute reality of death. Furnaces, lions' dens, the wrath of the inconstant, besotted king – no fictions these, but symbols striking home, then and now; the omnivorous empery, the demonic energy of death in the world.

In another place (Dan. 2:34–35) the initial "no" of the resisters is likened to a stone that gathers fierce momentum and eventually topples the superhuman image of the king. It is a stone that grows, a living stone; as alive as the "no" of resistance that echoes across a spiritual void. The stone grows to a monstrous boulder. Then it is launched, straight for its prey – the idolatrous image. The small stone becomes a very planet, a "no" large as the world. A "no" to idolatry and officially sanctioned violence. A "no" that also implies a "yes," the acceptance and welcoming of a new creation.

Daniel 1:17–21 The four companions, we are told, attain "wisdom" and "understanding" above their years, surpassing (more to the point!) all available wisdom of the king's court (Dan. 1:20). The gift is dangerous, apocalyptic; it announces a momentous event, altogether unexpected: the imminent end of the imperial order and the liberation of those who languish under its yoke.

Another arrow from the quiver of the afflicted; the story turns derisory. Minuscule respect, or none at all, is granted the eminences of the court. They are mocked without mercy, shown as clownish and capricious by turn. And the king? An unwitting buffoon, subject to chagrin and liverish change of mood. Broad-stroked caricatures, to be sure, and subversive of preposterous pomp and circumstance. (And an undoubted invitation for us to take a close, skeptical, even derisory look at the pretensions of the high and mighty. And in the task of resistance, to cultivate the good humor and high spirits that lighten oppression.)

On occasion, as the youths come to realize, the imperial method is murder, or seductive largesse (as in the enticements here held out). Daniel and his companions come to understand that both methods, for all their seeming contrast, are in reality one. The aim in each case is enslavement, enlistment in the tawdry imperial design.

Even as delicate viands are set grandly before them, they know that another, bitter menu is being shoved at their people. The young men, too, have tasted it – the food of exile. And the princely diet set before them is the fruit of murder and oppression.

So goes the logic whispered in the king's ear: Feed them well, O king; stuff them like capons. They will shortly become your sleek chattels. But the largehandedness of iron fist and velvet glove is all in vain. God bestows such wisdom upon her faithful ones.

The wisdom allows Daniel a longer perspective, as well. Defeat and humiliation surround his people, torn as they are from land and temple and tradition. Yet he foresees victory following defeat, and so announces an unprecedented outcome, literally beyond the imagining of most. The humiliated will rise again. Exile is not the last word, but return.

The chapter closes with a terse message of survival, Daniel's own, representing and presaging that of all. He lives on to see the fall of Babylon (Dan. 1:21). Indeed, under his gaze, at once courageous and insightful, the "victory" of the overlords collapses. They lose the game they presumed so easily to win. Their humiliating defeat is dramatized in the repeated failure of the "wise men" of the court to deliver on the king's demand; that they reconstruct his fantasies. (Strange that their "wisdom" fails them here; one can reasonably presume that their own dreams of glory would dovetail neatly with the king's.)

Enter Daniel, fasting, believing. It will shortly become clear that his wisdom is superior to all the wise. And we are privy once more to a theme of scripture: the conflict raging between two wisdoms, two insights; two versions, one might say, of the world and reality.

Isaiah issues a fierce diatribe against Pharaoh's crony counselors (Isa. 19). And Paul offers an extended contrast – on the one hand Hellenic forms of wisdom; on the other, the "foolishness" of the cross (1 Cor. 1:20 ff.).

In the present scene, there is simply no contest. We are in a realm of primary colors, an ancient drawing entitled "Daniel, Prevailing." Speedily the supposition that the young Jews are assimilated, beholden, "in service" to the king is shattered. Nothing of the kind. Their conscience is no commodity. Grasp of essentials, fidelity to covenant: these set them secretly – and then not secretly at all – apart.

How rarely, one reflects, does fidelity to God prevail among the servitors of kings. The common outcome is soberingly other.

Let us tell an old story. When such service is first undertaken, idealism reigns. The mind of the rising star is unclouded with doubts or second thoughts. High resolve and higher spirits are the order of the day. Rulers of whatever persuasion – kings, presidents – are presumed amenable to virtue. And for their part, many are persuaded that to "enter the system" is the optimum decision; when a person of high ideals enters the corridors of power, surely "things will change." Alas, the odds are stacked, and hardly in favor of such innocents, abroad or at home. The outcome, lamentably consistent, brings noble intentions to naught. The "system" coheres, a massive old boys' network of mutual stroking, of vagary, big money, guile, treachery, self interest, bunkum, low and high cunning – the system is adamant as oak, tough and durable. To say it brooks no interference is to understate its brute will to survive, if not prosper.

The neophyte thought, how fortunate I! to be in a position to speak the truth to power, a prophetic word, even a word of judgment. And to be taken seriously, obeyed.

But a genie is out of the bottle. Other influences and directions shortly take command, turning the best intentions to smoke and mirrors. We follow our high-minded counselor in his new eminence. He is easy and at home with the powerful, perhaps he takes his place at the king's table.

Is this latter proffer not evidence of the honor in which he is held? And ought he not respond with courtesy and acceptance? To do otherwise, to refuse the royal commensality, would be a bad beginning, a breach of good manners. (Whether scripture offers rules concerning the etiquette of this world is, of course, another matter.) Our well-intentioned friend sits to eat; he eats heartily and long. And in time he absorbs the atmosphere; he takes to parroting the talk that floats about the table, the gossip, cynicism, malice, mutual stroking.

Give him time. He will become the sedulous ape of those he fondly thought to instruct in altitudinous ways. He will sop up the etiquette, the abstractions and distractions and cabals and blood-ridden decisions. He will come to see the world through the gimlet lens of his royal patron, those wars ("necessary, just, forced on us"), that contempt for slaves and victims and prisoners. Like a young David, he will hearken to and harp away the royal distempers. He will take on the imperial mind as his own – that mind whose machinations dramatize the dynamics of the Fall.

Behold our quondam Galahad!* He has become a metronome, a clone of the powerful. A gear in the imperial machinery of necromancy, magic, and enchantment. In Camus'

*Galahad – the pure, noble, and unselfish hero of Arthurian fame.

terrible phrase, damning in its level tone of woe, he has become "like all the others."

Unlike Daniel. Our story might be entitled: Concerning One Who Walked The Thin Line. But never a word do we read concerning how to shine there, lockstep there, win there. Only the game itself, the dance, the taming of the beasts. And above all, the taming of the King of the beasts.

The Rock That Grew and Filled the Earth

The Book of Daniel

2 In the second year of Nebuchadnezzar's reign, Nebuchadnezzar dreamed such dreams that his spirit was troubled and
his sleep left him. 2So the king commanded that the magicians, the
enchanters, the sorcerers, and the Chaldeans be summoned to tell
the king his dreams. When they came in and stood before the king,
3he said to them, "I have had such a dream that my spirit is
troubled by the desire to understand it." 4The Chaldeans said to
the king (in Aramaic), "O king, live forever! Tell your servants the
dream, and we will reveal the interpretation." 5The king answered
the Chaldeans, "This is a public decree: if you do not tell me both
the dream and its interpretation, you shall be torn limb from limb,
and your houses shall be laid in ruins. 6But if you do tell me the
dream and its interpretation, you shall receive from me gifts and
rewards and great honor. Therefore tell me the dream and its interpretation." 7They answered a second time, "Let the king first tell
his servants the dream, then we can give its interpretation." 8The
king answered, "I know with certainty that you are trying to gain
time, because you see I have firmly decreed: 9if you do not tell me
the dream, there is but one verdict for you. You have agreed to
speak lying and misleading words to me until things take a turn.
Therefore, tell me the dream, and I shall know that you can give
me its interpretation." 10The Chaldeans answered the king, "There
is no one on earth who can reveal what the king demands! In fact
no king, however great and powerful, has ever asked such a thing of
any magician or enchanter or Chaldean. 11The thing that the king
is asking is too difficult, and no one can reveal it to the king except
the gods, whose dwelling is not with mortals."

12Because of this the king flew into a violent rage and commanded that all the wise men of Babylon be destroyed. 13The decree was issued, and the wise men were about to be executed; and
they looked for Daniel and his companions, to execute them.
14Then Daniel responded with prudence and discretion to Arioch,
the king's chief executioner, who had gone out to execute the wise

men of Babylon; [15]he asked Arioch, the royal official, "Why is the
decree of the king so urgent?" Arioch then explained the matter to
Daniel. [16]So Daniel went in and requested that the king give him
time and he would tell the king the interpretation.

[17]Then Daniel went to his home and informed his companions,
Hananiah, Mishael, and Azariah, [18]and told them to seek mercy
from the God of heaven concerning this mystery, so that Daniel
and his companions with the rest of the wise men of Babylon
might not perish. [19]Then the mystery was revealed to Daniel in a
vision of the night, and Daniel blessed the God of heaven.

[20]Daniel said:

"Blessed be the name of God from age to age,
  for wisdom and power are his.
[21]He changes times and seasons,
  deposes kings and sets up kings;
he gives wisdom to the wise
  and knowledge to those who have understanding.
[22]He reveals deep and hidden things;
  he knows what is in the darkness,
  and light dwells with him.
[23]To you, O God of my ancestors,
  I give thanks and praise,
for you have given me wisdom and power,
  and have now revealed to me what we asked of you,
for you have revealed to us what the king ordered."

[24]Therefore Daniel went to Arioch, whom the king had appointed
to destroy the wise men of Babylon, and said to him, "Do not destroy the wise men of Babylon; bring me in before the king, and I
will give the king the interpretation."

[25]Then Arioch quickly brought Daniel before the king and said
to him: "I have found among the exiles from Judah a man who can
tell the king the interpretation." [26]The king said to Daniel, whose
name was Belteshazzar, "Are you able to tell me the dream that I
have seen and its interpretation?" [27]Daniel answered the king, "No

wise men, enchanters, magicians, or diviners can show to the king
the mystery that the king is asking, 28but there is a God in heaven
who reveals mysteries, and he has disclosed to King Nebuchadnezzar what will happen at the end of days. Your dream and the visions
of your head as you lay in bed were these: 29To you, O king, as you
lay in bed, came thoughts of what would be hereafter, and the
revealer of mysteries disclosed to you what is to be. 30But as for me,
this mystery has not been revealed to me because of any wisdom
that I have more than any other living being, but in order that the
interpretation may be known to the king and that you may understand the thoughts of your mind.

31"You were looking, O king, and lo! there was a great statue.
This statue was huge, its brilliance extraordinary; it was standing
before you, and its appearance was frightening. 32The head of that
statue was of fine gold, its chest and arms of silver, its middle and
thighs of bronze, 33its legs of iron, its feet partly of iron and partly
of clay. 34As you looked on, a stone was cut out, not by human
hands, and it struck the statue on its feet of iron and clay and broke
them in pieces. 35Then the iron, the clay, the bronze, the silver, and
the gold, were all broken in pieces and became like the chaff of the
summer threshing floors; and the wind carried them away, so that
not a trace of them could be found. But the stone that struck the
statue became a great mountain and filled the whole earth.

36"This was the dream; now we will tell the king its interpretation. 37You, O king, the king of kings – to whom the God of heav-
en has given the kingdom, the power, the might, and the glory,
38into whose hand he has given human beings, wherever they live,
the wild animals of the field, and the birds of the air, and whom he
has established as ruler over them all – you are the head of gold.
39After you shall arise another kingdom inferior to yours, and yet a
third kingdom of bronze, which shall rule over the whole earth.
40And there shall be a fourth kingdom, strong as iron; just as iron
crushes and smashes everything, it shall crush and shatter all these.
41As you saw the feet and toes partly of potter's clay and partly of
iron, it shall be a divided kingdom; but some of the strength of iron

shall be in it, as you saw the iron mixed with the clay. [42]As the toes of the feet were part iron and part clay, so the kingdom shall be partly strong and partly brittle. [43]As you saw the iron mixed with clay, so will they mix with one another in marriage, but they will not hold together, just as iron does not mix with clay. [44]And in the days of those kings the God of heaven will set up a kingdom that shall never be destroyed, nor shall this kingdom be left to another people. It shall crush all these kingdoms and bring them to an end, and it shall stand forever; [45]just as you saw that a stone was cut from the mountain not by hands, and that it crushed the iron, the bronze, the clay, the silver, and the gold. The great God has informed the king what shall be hereafter. The dream is certain, and its interpretation trustworthy."

[46]Then King Nebuchadnezzar fell on his face, worshiped Daniel, and commanded that a grain offering and incense be offered to him. [47]The king said to Daniel, "Truly, your God is God of gods and Lord of kings and a revealer of mysteries, for you have been able to reveal this mystery!" [48]Then the king promoted Daniel, gave him many great gifts, and made him ruler over the whole province of Babylon and chief prefect over all the wise men of Babylon. [49]Daniel made a request of the king, and he appointed Shadrach, Meshach, and Abednego over the affairs of the province of Babylon. But Daniel remained at the king's court.

The Rock That Grew and Filled the Earth

Daniel 2:1–12 We enter upon a famous sequence. Famous especially, one thinks, for its tone of overt mockery. (That saving humor of the oppressed! Under its barrage the great ones totter on their pedestals and fall flat, overbearing as they are, and formidable and absurd as the images they concoct!)

Here Daniel is presented as interpreter, through divine inspiration, of the king's dream. (Later he will be shown as a formidable dreamer on his own account.)

There is a question, both haunting and humorous, surrounding the royal farrago. Namely, did the king himself remember his dream? If we presume he did, we have a clue as to his testy treatment of the magic men. He alone, after all, is in a position to judge their confabulations, since he alone holds the key to the dream. So he can judge whether the necromancers are delivering – or duping – him.

If, on the other hand, we presume that the king forgot his dream and is here demanding its entire reconstruction, we have another sort of clue; this time, to the extraordinarily nimble mind of Daniel.

From his agility proceed one or perhaps two feats, equally wonderful. Let us suppose that he does reconstruct the king's fantasies on demand. Or this: taking the measure of the king with devastating accuracy, royal ego and all, he constructs out of thin air and inspired soul a plausible dream.

Let us concede something to the embattled court magians. It must be admitted that the regal test is unimaginably cruel and arbitrary. With no hint offered as to subject or theme, they are to confabulate the king's somatic dream sequence. If they succeed, honors and riches galore await. And if they fail? It is, as one might put the dilemma, the worst imperial catch-22.

Over against them Daniel is greatly advantaged. He is cognizant of the great dream times of the Bible, of the great dreamers as well, and of those who interpreted skillfully and thus enlightened the tribe. Dreams and dreamers! Like a crowded ark afloat against odds in the storms of history – the Bible positively teems with them. There is Jacob and the dream of a promised land (Gen. 28:12 ff.). And much resembling Daniel, there is Joseph and his dangerous dreams of prevailing over his brothers (Gen. 37:5–11). With consummate skill, he brings the Pharaoh through his troubled nightmares (Gen. 41:39 ff.). Solomon, too, receives divine wisdom through a dream (1 Kings 3:5 ff.).

Our New Testament bears witness to visions and visionaries as well. Joseph, a practical man, is a carpenter; yet how vivid his dream life! At the start he is angelically enlightened as to the marvels proceeding in the person of his lady, Mary. She is betrothed to the Holy Spirit, and impregnated by the Divine One (Matt. 1:20). The holy child is born, and a murderous Herod seeks his death. Joseph is warned in a dream to take the child and his mother and flee to Egypt (Matt. 2:13).

And in the early church, Luke offers a kind of mutuality of dreams and dreamers. A complex interplay of images brings together the apostle Peter and a Roman centurion named Cornelius, the seeker and the sought. The story occupies the entire tenth chapter of Acts, a testimony of its import to the nascent community. The Jewish mold is breaking apart; the world of gentiles is at the door, seeking entrance to the new community. An honored outsider, one described as "religious and godfearing," turns Christward.

Back to the strange encounter between the king, his stalemated vizards, and Daniel. A thundrous double command is issued. First, tell the king his dream; second, interpret it! Our hero witnesses with a measure of sympathy the confusion and dread of the Chaldean wizards. "Never" is their anguished wail; and no wonder, for never in the memory of human history was a like command issued.

Daniel 2:13–23 The king is a berserker, his illogic a scythe in mad hands, cutting a relentless swath. And Daniel appears in person for the first time. He and his friends unaccountably fall under the decree entitled "dream time or death." Why? Such stories as these hardly arise in praise of the good sense of kings, let alone in praise of their justice.

Thus early in the book we are treated to an example – heavy handed, satiric, mocking the great one. Shall we call it the "view from beneath?" The glance of an exiled community falls like a rapier on imperial pretensions. Piquant, this humor of the oppressed, and saving at that!

A dire decree has been issued. Daniel must act with circumspection (Dan. 2:13). And speedily. He proceeds with great good sense, first seeking a restraining order, and then approaching the king. A final errand takes him back to his companions, where he urges on them a crucial charge – prayer.

We have at length both our setting and its actors. Exiles, survivors, the little community of Daniel, disciplined, lucid, strongly given to fasting and prayer. A kind of "base community." And now they are under further duress.

They fall to prayer. Simply, faith drives them; recourse will bring relief. And at all cost they must not allow evil to separate them from God, whose holy love and mercy grants endurance. Thus, too, Daniel's behavior in the breach comes as a brusque reminder; the need in us, too, of such mindfulness as is here commended.

Other times, like needs? Our times, largely bereft of a sense of God, press down on us like a millstone. Our culture pushes hard its own version of the good life, success, appetite fulfilled, prowess, primacy of place. The images are of great force, relentlessly enticing and seductive. They are also despairing, debased, suffused with greed and violence, with racism, sexism, with the "legitimacy" and "justness"of war and abortion, the death penalty and assisted suicide. And what of life – life as gift and joy and access to innocence and wisdom, whether of young or aged? Life is cheap. It is expendable, and ridden with necrophilia. In certain "cases" it were best ended, we are told, in favor of an outcome beneficial to all concerned: death. Thus is eroded to the vanishing point our sense of God and of one another.

Were such a version of human life to prevail, the spiritual descendants of Daniel would in effect fall prey to the spurious wisdom of the king's court, with all its implications intact – the lure of despair, recourse to magic, power on the prowl.

No; yet another No. Daniel insists that prayer alone will reveal what he terms the "mystery." The word itself is mysterious and offered without elaboration. Recurring as it does throughout the book, the "mystery" is of obvious import to the author. Here the word bears the weight of the secret dream of the king. And for us Christians, far more. It anticipates the richer sense of the word as developed by Paul (Eph. 3). In brief, the "mystery" in Daniel becomes for Christians the Mystery. Thus we have a synonym for Christ, the Mystery summing up and summoning to himself all mysteries, the Code Name, the divine-human one, Emmanuel, God among us, on behalf of us, in favor of us; the accessible, vulnerable, valiant Eirenicon.*

*Eirenicon – (Gr.) "bringer of reconciliation."

But to our story. Early on, a common theme emerges. Kings are enthroned on high, for that is the way of the world. But: the same eminences can be dethroned, brought low with astonishing ease. And that is the way of the Bible. And the lowly, for their part, are exalted and vindicated.

Thus a final act nears, or at least becomes less unlikely. In the unfolding drama of history, such spectacular reversals of fortune signal a nascent movement. A faint stirring, a slight tremor of earth. Or something barely visible, a prelude, a predawn, just over the rim of time. Then, momentous, irresistible – the sun, the onset of God's realm!

One does not announce the Event easily or lightly. What comes to be known as the Day of Jahweh is lighted by a sun that rises but knows no setting. Watch, therefore, and be vigilant. That Day is preceded by a "day of testing" for such as Daniel and his community. For every believing community.

The testing is secular to the hilt, classic. It is also ominously familiar to the mindful and courageous. No king in history but yields place with wrathful resistance, a fury that may seek the death of such as challenge or seek to supplant. Daniel and his like are prepared for the day of testing, that fearsome inaugural of the Unveiling. For this reason prepared, they have been frequently at prayer.

So Daniel also is granted his dream. And a dream within his dream; the king's dream, revealed.

Daniel 2:20 The community lies under an ominous shadow, the royal threat, wild and wide ranging. And they fall to prayer. The prayer is a pastiche of scriptural literacy: Daniel draws on the Psalms, Job, Exodus, Habakkuk, Ezekiel, Isaiah. It pleads not solely for personal deliverance but shows a sense of public trust, compassion, and responsibility.

In the long run Daniel's resolve is the salvation and well-being of his people. But he concentrates for the moment on those in immediate danger. We note his compassion; he would pluck from summary death even his adversaries, the magicians.

The prayer (Dan. 2:20–23) is carefully transcribed; one has a sense of word-for-word import, as though it were being underscored for our sake. As though we were invited to make it our prayer? It rewards a close look. It opens with a blessing, a Jewish liturgical form honored also by Paul and indeed by Jesus in time of crisis.

It might occur as strange that we humans feel moved to "bless" the blessed One. The formula is perhaps best taken as a word of simple, heartfelt acknowledgment. It bespeaks a pause, an attentive hearkening, a break in routine. Perhaps it implies, too, that a crisis is at hand – and then a breakthrough, long sought, imminent. Is one in trouble, at the end of his rope, as Daniel and his friends, in this episode? It were commonsensical to pause, take stock, implore relief.

Daniel utters a word of praise, of acknowledging. So doing, he casts off a kind of fatalism, almost an agnosticism, the taken-for-granted attitude of the unheeding (including heedless rulers) toward reality – one's own, the creation itself. Among such, boredom rules. We are where we are in the world and time; it is all dead, two dimensional, "out of our hands," flat and featureless, a "given." Routine (including the routine of empire) stifles questions, becomes our magister, our only recourse.

Daniel is no gull. He is not easily deceived, hardly assimilated to those named (with more than a soupçon of contempt) "dwellers upon the earth." Which is to say, those who dwell nowhere else. Prisoners of time, like characters in a Beckett play, stuck in "that which is seen," in recurrent follies and graceless gravity.

No to all that! Daniel's life touches the bedrock of reality. Say it then, joyous and strong: praise for that gift, for creation, for life itself! (Need one add that such a word of praise would never occur to the king or his cohorts?)

The prayer, the praise, these overcome. They bespeak freedom from a normalcy that destroys and defeats. In that dead zone life drags on, at the mercy of presumption; creation (as we claim it for our own, food, lodging, the earth we walk, the shape and tenor of the world's seasons, its glorious nights and days) – all this is set in place and handed over, we know not how, we have no care to ask why or how. The cornucopia tips in our direction; goodness and beauty pour out. All taken for granted, simply "our due." Why question or give thanks? People, too, taken for granted: friends, spouses, children.

All is at my service in sum, and no heed paid, no response welling up. The world, so to speak, being self-explained, self-enclosed, and I explained and enclosed within its sheath. Like a corpse wrapped in its shroud, or a pupa in a cocoon. Or dead – before birth.

None of this with Daniel. A grace, the "blessing" is uttered. Daniel turns to the "God of Heaven." Thus verse 20. The "blessing" proceeds. His gaze wide ranging, Daniel looks before and after. Indeed, standing before God without carnal history, Daniel stands in the line of those who bless "from age to age." This is his truest ancestry – those who, having been blessed, utter blessings. A passionate hope is also implied: that he hand on the blessing to the unborn.

To God belong "wisdom and strength." The implication is deliciously subtle. Wisdom and strength are cardinal needs of the community, given the testing that lies so close. To praise God for them, then, is to entreat on behalf of the supplicants these same gifts. We pray: What You are, grant us, that we may be rendered godly.

Daniel, artful before the king, is artful before God. He refuses a false, unlikely role. He will not appear before the Holy as deprived, childish, or artless; powerless, cap-in-hand. The prayer is mature, it issues from a heart well tested. He seeks virtues apt to adulthood.

Daniel 2:21–22 The description of God proceeds. Through God, "seasons and times" go on, though in a manner consonant with our freedom (whether it be celebrated or abused).

There is a vivid contrast to be noted here, again by implication (Daniel is a master of indirection; another tool of the oppressed). According to Babylonian theology, we humans are blind, bound ineluctably to a wheel of fortune and misfortune, playthings of the gods. All but the kings are thus fated to be born, live, and die. The only exception is offered these great ones, the rulers and their votaries, divinely favored. Favored, we ask? Is this king, besotted and dudgeonous by turn – to be called free? The Daniel story mocks in outrageous episodes his peevishness and guile; mocks as well a theology that would exalt so vast a nonentity. Thus the sweet revenge of the underdog.

The believing community stands before an unbelieving king. And for this dark majesty, Daniel and his friends might rightly be termed an only hope. The wisdom of Daniel is rightly seen as a public gift. It is offered on behalf of one benighted and needful. An emperor unclothed – and disclosed as such. Indeed, what chance of salvation, of granting truth a place in the royal court, except Daniel be true to his call, embracing the chancy, dangerous vocation of truth-teller? Deprived of Daniel, the king, chafed and fractious, would suffer a fate worse than the death he has decreed for his minions. He would be condemned to the hell of his own dream. Condemned to "what is in the darkness" (Dan 2:22).

Daniel's friends are messengers, but their message is hardly received as a welcome one. It goes something like this: Kings, too, are mortal; you too, high and mighty though you be, will die.

A Hand touches the regal shoulder. The scepter falls; the king's hand is stricken nerveless. The blow is a summons: You are in no way exempt from the common fate. Rise then, flourish for awhile, and die. Do you resist, persuaded that you exceed the common lot of birth and death, of prospering and sorrow? The gesture renders the pretension null.

Thus the great ones fall from their thrones. Others, in sum neither better nor worse, sycophants, soothsayers, would-be heirs, fueled by ambition and greed, scramble after the scepter. And the God of Daniel witnesses it all; dare we say smiles a secret smile?

As we have suggested, the deflation of overweening pride is the tone of our book. More, the like theme is a commonplace in the prophetic books. In this task Daniel stands in the line of those who shake the thrones, who warn the mighty: There are limits, boundaries, caveats. Exceed them not.

This, it would seem, is the ultimate refinement and luster of the prophetic call: Daniel accepts responsibility, even for the fate of the persecutor. Thus his prophetic actions, mimes, words and parables raise a mighty prayer of intercession, a plea on behalf of the tyrant.

So in our day. Perhaps a personal vignette would be of point here. A decade or more ago, my brother Philip and I were locked in a cell in a Washington, D.C. jail, after a demonstration at the White House. Among questions that rose to my mind as we pondered the scriptures was this: How describe our responsibility toward those who were in effect criminalizing and punishing us? What possible good might we be offering on behalf of say, Messrs. Reagan and Kissinger, who dwelt in a somewhat different ambiance across town? I well remember Philip's response. He said simply: I think we are their only hope.

The prayer of Daniel is subtly subversive. Favorable outcome or disastrous, royal change of heart or none, the truth has been stated. To wit, the king is subject to judgment.

A wonderful contrast is offered. Kings, by presumption, are gifted with wisdom. Or so it is said. Their wisdom is strongly endorsed by others – men skilled in state craft, surrogates, advisers, counselors whose wisdom is constantly at the king's ear. Often the arrangement, the communality of interest, holds firm for a time. Which is to say, the king and his court dream a like dream.

Yet now and again, as in the present episode, everything falls apart. Such a scheme of things, the conjuring and conjunction of power, breaks in pieces. The book of Daniel is clear on the point: limits, strict boundaries are set about worldly wisdom. Thus the prophets speak without exception. The king and his cronies, know it or not, are in service to "the system," to structural sinfulness.

In later times, Thomas Aquinas will formulate the same two-edged idea: grace presupposes and builds on (really leans on) nature. If the "nature" be corrupt, willful, unjust, or violent, grace is stopped short, stalemated. The gift of God is rendered null and void. More often than is admitted, the powerful offer little of substance for grace to infuse and enlighten. There is only "the system" and their subjection to it. Its marks are greed, recourse to violence, moral blindness, incapacity and pride of place bizarrely conjoined.

"God gives wisdom to the wise." Still we reflect how frequently in Daniel's time and our own such wisdom is humiliated, suspect, put to naught, legally prosecuted, even done to death. And short of this fate, how often the truly wise walk the earth as strangers, aliens, "illegals" exerting little or no weight in the scales of power.

Now and again (so rarely), an epiphany is accorded. As in the story of Daniel, a momentary glory shines, invites, an avatar. Back, forth the ray of light ranges, Daniel to the king. And the divine wisdom concentrates like a burning glass on the semblances and pretensions of the powerful. The truth combusts. Smoke, and then flame.

Careful, Daniel, this king is volatile. Like a mad Saul or a Lear, his dark mood will return, eroding heart and mind, bringing darkness in its wake. Thus the habitual estate of Daniel and his friends is by no means an abiding or trustworthy royal favor. Their true circumstance is endangerment.

Daniel 2:23 ff. The prayer is ended, and the granting of its plea is announced. It is simple as that. The "wisdom and strength" of God dwell in Daniel; he is ready for the testing of wisdom and strength. One has a sense of calm self-possession. God is with the resisters; then who shall oppose them? Take me to the king.

Again, "the mystery." And the waters deepen and darken. Daniel's revelation will center not only on a capital event of the immediate future, the downfall of Babylon. It encompasses "what will come to pass in the last days."

Indeed mysterious: What is to come, what form will be taken by that new, momentous reality? The question is taken up explicitly (Dan. 2:44). Coming on a day known only to God is a reign of an entirely different order, beyond the grasp of empires, beyond their wise ones, the run of their citizenry – even, for the most, part beyond the ken of their victims and slaves. According to Jews and Christians, the new reality is the Reign of God on earth. For Christians, it will be announced and instigated by Jesus.

In pledge of this, the Savior will take to himself an extraordinary title. It is conferred in a vision accorded to Daniel 7; the "Human One" (or "Son of Man"). We shall dwell upon it later. Jesus will also seize on the "rock" image (see Dan. 3; also Isa. 28:16 and Ps. 118:22). And Revelation 1:1, 19, and 4:1 borrow the term "what will come to pass…" Thus the imagery of Daniel, germinal and lustrous with life, passes through Hebrew and Christian bible as a single, subtle thread of gold. The same images are found repeatedly on the lips of the holy ones, midrash after midrash.

Daniel 2:30 "This mystery…revealed to me" (that word again!) "that you may know the thoughts of your own heart." It would seem that penetration of the "mystery" is joined closely with self knowledge.

Maybe the times demand it, that our claims remain modest, even minimal. That at the same time, we know and give thanks; something hidden from the great ones of this world is known to us. We are granted a measure of access to the "mystery."

Is this one aspect of the "mystery" known to the faithful – our conviction that such events as appall and would drag us down, are not the whole of reality? The great ones of our lifetime lay waste to creation in servitude to war. They oppress and slay, play like pagan godlings with the lives of widows and orphans.

Those who take meat from the table
Teach contentment.
Those for whom the contribution is destined
Demand sacrifice.
Those who eat to the fill speak to the hungry
Of wonderful times to come.
Those who lead the country into the abyss
Call ruling too difficult
For ordinary men.

Those at the top say:
This way to glory.
Those down below say:
This way to the grave.
Bertolt Brecht, From a German War Primer

To speak of ourselves, we repeat to our own soul and to one another, through prayer and sacrament, a mantra: "The kings are mortal, the kings stand under judgment." They remain profoundly ignorant of such truths. They lay claim to a spurious immortality; they presume to stand under no judgment, to be a law unto themselves. And the truth tellers pay tribute to the gift, the wisdom, the mystery, "not through any wisdom of mine..."

Daniel 2:31–35 That royal dream – it could take only one form. The king dreams of the king. And the dream is pure nightmare, for it is truthful. Head to foot, this is what the imperial one is made of; his image is a monstrous hodgepodge of gold and baser matter. Regal, as befits his majesty, the gold is also larcenous, pilfered from the earth, from enemies, from bribe and ransom. The head is crowned and bears the king's own features, as is meet and just. Down and down the eye follows – to the feet, where indeed the heaviest weight must be borne. And the feet are fired in shifty clay and iron, elements which, as Daniel understands, simply refuse to mix.

What (better, who) is to bear the weight of all this glory? Why are not the feet, indeed the entire colossus, made of gold? Is not the king kingly throughout? Or if the feet are not of gold, why are they not of a material apt to tolerate the tremendous weight bearing down?

As noted, the feet are of a curious mix, clay and iron. Thus is implied the truth of the dream, the "mystery" which "makes kings to tumble, kings to rise." Death and judgment once more, the "mystery" inaccessible to his highness. The king is vulnerable, his footing unsure; he sways ever so slightly, then greatly. And then, alas, he tumbles.

Subversive the truth, and long withheld; and the skills, the cunning of counselors, these are brought up short. Isaiah offers a cruder image; but his status is less vulnerable than Daniel's. The "wise of this world," he avers, "are drunk... they reel in their own vomit" (Isa. 19:14.). The truth is told outright. And for a change, hope is in the air. Against all odds, even a tyrant may mend his unsavory ways.

Daniel 2:36–43 Three kingdoms will succeed the Babylonian: the Persian, Greek, and Roman. These will eventually fade to a diminishing power and grandeur. Still, a caveat: The fourth, the feet – Rome – is a diehard, capable (Dan. 2: 40) of "crushing, reducing all to powder."

Worthy of note also that the "fourth kingdom" is interpreted far differently by Jews. According to their midrash, this "fourth" signifies not the Roman empire, but the church in the centuries after Constantine. The Christians, newly endorsed as the "official religion," hasten to make common cause with the empire that has welcomed them. The newly installed religion eclipses the secular order in power and grandeur. And shortly the murderous persecution of Jews is underway, with the sanction of church and state.

Daniel 2:44–45 There comes at long last a fifth realm, its symbol a rock whose rule will be everlasting, its sovereignty passing to no other. And its splendor will surpass all previous realms and principalities.

The rock is engendered in a dream; it is of another world than ours. A waking sense could hardly verify its wild ways. It is as though a lavic explosion had cast an entire continent to the surface, white hot. Born from the depths of the unconscious? This rock is conscious; it gathers to itself qualities as it pleases. It is "cut out by no human hand." It is alive, it grows and grows, from within, to the magnitude of a mountain. Thundrously, imagine! It strains up and up, until it claims high heaven.

Now it includes and subsumes all of creation. It becomes a very world, the only world, the eventual world, the final form of all things, of all worlds. This, then, would seem to be implied, by way of summary. Unto itself, final, definitive, of God, nothing can supplant the rock nor anticipate it, nor presume to possess it. No power or principality or empire or military or economic or religious power avails to sway it from its appointment with destiny and destiny's God. Nothing can allow or forbid it place, or dictate its form or duration.

This being so, something momentous follows. No conceivable political, economic, even "religious" arrangement, of whatever brilliance, scope, benevolence, valiance can announce itself or be hailed by enthusiasts as the Realm of God. No such thing. The living, growing, subsuming rock is a being of an entirely different order.

Imagination boggles, words fail; we cast up our hands and murmur something about an "act of God." A sorry response, but the best we can come upon. No mortal has seen the like. How then summon, imagine the rock, its form, its amplitude, its humanity? How place our existence within it?

A second thought. Let us modify the above confession: it is too dire. We have seen something of the like. And have striven as best we might to live in accord with the Manifesto of the Mountain, and to seek its blessings (Matt. 5).

Thus here and there from the living rock spring forth sons and daughters received into full citizenry of the Realm of the rock: the poor, the meek, the pure of heart. These are the forerunners of human transformation; they dwell not upon the earth, not stuck in time and place, as though shadows and images were all of reality. They account world and time as a mere sojourn, "a night in an uncomfortable inn" (Teresa of Avila). Often as not, they dwell in prison.

My Brother's Battered Bible,
Carried Repeatedly into Prison

That book
livid with thumb prints,
underscorings, lashes –
I see you carry it
into the cave of storms, past the storms.
I see you underscore

like the score of music
all that travail
that furious unexplained joy.

Contraband! the guards
seize, shake it out –
the apostles wail, the women
breathe deep as Cumaean sibyls,
Herod screams like a souped-up record.
They toss it back, harmless.
Now, seated on a cell bunk
you play the pages slowly, slowly,
a lifeline humming with the song
of the jeweled fish, all but taken.

D. B.

Let us take another tack – that of a politically fervent, secular hope. Let us imagine for a moment an improbable event. A newborn political entity has taken power after a protracted struggle. It is manifestly superior, both to the system it replaced and to surrounding systems; it is praiseworthy and plausible, humane, truthful, nonviolent, ardent in pursuit of justice and compassion. By multitudes within and without, the regime is hailed with quasi-religious fervor. Religious folk go further; they proclaim that the admirable new order signals the onset of the realm of God.

Such has occurred in our time (perhaps it occurs periodically, as the apogee of a cycle of despair-hope). It is the religious imagery that offends – the finality of it, the banality, the attempt to seize on the meaning of the "end time" – the denial, in effect, of the Fall, and its ironbound hold on time and this world. Such a claim, it would seem, betrays the intent of our text (not to speak of numerous other texts making the identical point). Finality belongs to God.

The rock is an image of preeminence. It nullifies all other images of power, all kingdoms, no matter how lowly (those feet of clay) or grandiose (the head, crowned, of gold). The image also implies a considerable violence. In such a world as ours, the rock strikes hard.

It takes to itself the anger of Christ, confronting as it must (and as he must) hardness of heart, claims and counterclaims of omnipotence, worldly systems, whether of church or state, their pretensions, ruthlessness, legalism, violence, contempt for the victims they themselves create, their blindness and folly. Another, a greater than Daniel, has said, "The violent bear it [the Realm] away."

The image of the rock implies an invitation and urging. In our times we are invited to consider (and to undertake) startling forms of nonviolent activity. To set the rock rolling, striking against self-deifying images of authority. To confront the law that legitimates such images and declares them beyond critique, even worthy of reverence; that creates a citizenry of mute obeisants. To the crowned heads, let us offer the truth. The truth includes this: the feet are of clay. Let us offer the same truth to those who yield and fall to knee: the feet are of clay.

Such actions strike hard against consecrated, stereotyped ways and means, icons that have become idols, lying images, masks laid upon dark motives. How hard such nonviolence strikes! We have seen it – blank incomprehension and official fury follow on such actions. The actions strike hard also against numbed faith and mute acceptance of evil as inevitable, invincible, turning to water the courage of mere mortals.

The times, our times, who shall tell of them, diagnose them? Their politics, their economics, their official, human sense, in many instances their religion – these are to be accounted, by any standard available to the sane, as far gone in lunacy. They are numb, necrophiliac, hallucinatory, grisly, somnambulistic, morally cramped and ferociously cruel.

A symptom of the above, a clue: among many Christians, such deadly idols as nuclear weapons raise not a whiff of scandal. But what a storm and scandal erupt when a few Christians decide to launch a "rock" against these images of violence!

The scandal is strangely misapplied, one thinks, when nuclear weapons are regarded as normal and civil disobedience as scandalous. So turning reality on its head, allowing place for such monstrous weaponry amid fair creation, Christians accord to obscenities a form of debased worship.

A song goes, "For swords into plowshares, the hammer has to fall." Which is to say, for bringing down the idolatrous image, the rock must be set rolling.

Daniel 2:46 We are told of an outcome large with hope. As Daniel's exegesis of the dream ends, the king is converted. It seems as though the compassion and wisdom of the seer have exorcised the royal demons; the dream has been stripped of its obsessive power. Thus too the liberating lesson is driven home; Jahweh alone is God. The episode closes; it is favorable to Daniel and Daniel's God. And most unexpectedly, by a near miraculous grace, favorable to the tyrant as well.

A final note. That Daniel would allow sacrifices and oblations to be offered to himself has proven embarrassing. Some talmudic texts reprove the great man for this. And, it would seem, rightly so.

Who Shall Perish, and Who Be Delivered

The Book of Daniel

3 King Nebuchadnezzar made a golden statue whose height was sixty cubits and whose width was six cubits; he set it up on the plain of Dura in the province of Babylon. 2Then King Nebuchadnezzar sent for the satraps, the prefects, and the governors, the counselors, the treasurers, the justices, the magistrates, and all the officials of the provinces to assemble and come to the dedication of the statue that King Nebuchadnezzar had set up. 3So the satraps, the prefects, and the governors, the counselors, the treasurers, the justices, the magistrates, and all the officials of the provinces, assembled for the dedication of the statue that King Nebuchadnezzar had set up. When they were standing before the statue that Nebuchadnezzar had set up, 4the herald proclaimed aloud, "You are commanded, O peoples, nations, and languages, 5that when you hear the sound of the horn, pipe, lyre, trigon, harp, drum, and entire musical ensemble, you are to fall down and worship the golden statue that King Nebuchadnezzar has set up. 6Whoever does not fall down and worship shall immediately be thrown into a furnace of blazing fire." 7Therefore, as soon as all the peoples heard the sound of the horn, pipe, lyre, trigon, harp, drum, and entire musical ensemble, all the peoples, nations, and languages fell down and worshiped the golden statue that King Nebuchadnezzar had set up.

8Accordingly, at this time certain Chaldeans came forward and denounced the Jews. 9They said to King Nebuchadnezzar, "O king, live forever! 10You, O king, have made a decree, that everyone who hears the sound of the horn, pipe, lyre, trigon, harp, drum, and entire musical ensemble, shall fall down and worship the golden statue, 11and whoever does not fall down and worship shall be thrown into a furnace of blazing fire. 12There are certain Jews whom you have appointed over the affairs of the province of Babylon: Shadrach, Meshach, and Abednego. These pay no heed to you, O King. They do not serve your gods and they do not worship the golden statue that you have set up."

13Then Nebuchadnezzar in furious rage commanded that Shadrach, Meshach, and Abednego be brought in; so they brought those men before the king. [14]Nebuchadnezzar said to them, "Is it true, O Shadrach, Meshach, and Abednego, that you do not serve my gods and you do not worship the golden statue that I have set up? [15]Now if you are ready when you hear the sound of the horn, pipe, lyre, trigon, harp, drum, and entire musical ensemble to fall down and worship the statue that I have made, well and good. But if you do not worship, you shall immediately be thrown into a furnace of blazing fire, and who is the god that will deliver you out of my hands?"

[16]Shadrach, Meshach, and Abednego answered the king, "O Nebuchadnezzar, we have no need to present a defense to you in this matter. [17]If our God whom we serve is able to deliver us from the furnace of blazing fire and out of your hand, O king, let him deliver us. [18]But if not, be it known to you, O king, that we will not serve your gods and we will not worship the golden statue that you have set up."

[19]Then Nebuchadnezzar was so filled with rage against Shadrach, Meshach, and Abednego that his face was distorted. He ordered the furnace heated up seven times more than was customary, [20]and ordered some of the strongest guards in his army to bind Shadrach, Meshach, and Abednego and to throw them into the furnace of blazing fire. [21]So the men were bound, still wearing their tunics, their trousers, their hats, and their other garments, and they were thrown into the furnace of blazing fire. [22]Because the king's command was urgent and the furnace was so overheated, the raging flames killed the men who lifted Shadrach, Meshach, and Abednego. [23]But the three men, Shadrach, Meshach, and Abednego, fell down, bound, into the furnace of blazing fire.

[24]Then King Nebuchadnezzar was astonished and rose up quickly. He said to his counselors, "Was it not three men that we threw bound into the fire?" They answered the king, "True, O king." [25]He replied, "But I see four men unbound, walking in the middle of the fire, and they are not hurt; and the fourth has the appearance of a god." [26]Nebuchadnezzar then approached the door

of the furnace of blazing fire and said, "Shadrach, Meshach, and
Abednego, servants of the Most High God, come out! Come here!"
So Shadrach, Meshach, and Abednego came out from the fire.
27And the satraps, the prefects, the governors, and the king's counselors gathered together and saw that the fire had not had any
power over the bodies of those men; the hair of their heads was not
singed, their tunics were not harmed, and not even the smell of fire
came from them. 28Nebuchadnezzar said, "Blessed be the God of
Shadrach, Meshach, and Abednego, who has sent his angel and delivered his servants who trusted in him. They disobeyed the king's
command and yielded up their bodies rather than serve and worship any god except their own God. 29Therefore I make a decree:
Any people, nation, or language that utters blasphemy against the
God of Shadrach, Meshach, and Abednego shall be torn limb from
limb, and their houses laid in ruins; for there is no other god who is
able to deliver in this way." 30Then the king promoted Shadrach,
Meshach, and Abednego in the province of Babylon.

4 King Nebuchadnezzar to all peoples, nations, and languages
that live throughout the earth: May you have abundant prosperity! 2The signs and wonders that the Most High God has
worked for me I am pleased to recount.

3How great are his signs,
how mighty his wonders!
His kingdom is an everlasting kingdom,
and his sovereignty is from generation to generation.

4I, Nebuchadnezzar, was living at ease in my home and prospering
in my palace. 5I saw a dream that frightened me; my fantasies in
bed and the visions of my head terrified me. 6So I made a decree
that all the wise men of Babylon should be brought before me, in
order that they might tell me the interpretation of the dream.
7Then the magicians, the enchanters, the Chaldeans, and the diviners came in, and I told them the dream, but they could not tell
me its interpretation. 8At last Daniel came in before me – he who

was named Belteshazzar after the name of my god, and who is endowed with a spirit of the holy gods – and I told him the dream:
9"O Belteshazzar, chief of the magicians, I know that you are
endowed with a spirit of the holy gods and that no mystery is
too difficult for you. Hear the dream that I saw; tell me its interpretation.

10Upon my bed this is what I saw;
there was a tree at the center of the earth,
and its height was great.
11The tree grew great and strong,
its top reached to heaven,
and it was visible to the ends of the whole earth.
12Its foliage was beautiful,
its fruit abundant,
and it provided food for all.
The animals of the field found shade under it,
the birds of the air nested in its branches,
and from it all living beings were fed.

13I continued looking, in the visions of my head as I lay in bed, and
there was a holy watcher, coming down from heaven. 14He cried
aloud and said:

'Cut down the tree and chop off its branches,
strip off its foliage and scatter its fruit.
Let the animals flee from beneath it
and the birds from its branches.
15But leave its stump and roots in the ground,
with a band of iron and bronze,
in the tender grass of the field.
Let him be bathed with the dew of heaven,
and let his lot be with the animals of the field
in the grass of the earth.
16Let his mind be changed from that of a human,
and let the mind of an animal be given to him.
And let seven times pass over him.

17 The sentence is rendered by decree of the watchers,
    the decision is given by order of the holy ones,
in order that all who live may know that
    the Most High is sovereign over the kingdom of mortals;
he gives it to whom he will
    and sets over it the lowliest of human beings.'

18 This is the dream that I, King Nebuchadnezzar, saw. Now you,
Belteshazzar, declare the interpretation, since all the wise men of
my kingdom are unable to tell me the interpretation. You are able,
however, for you are endowed with a spirit of the holy gods."

19 Then Daniel, who was called Belteshazzar, was severely distressed for a while. His thoughts terrified him. The king said,
"Belteshazzar, do not let the dream or the interpretation terrify
you." Belteshazzar answered, "My lord, may the dream be for those
who hate you, and its interpretation for your enemies! 20 The tree
that you saw, which grew great and strong, so that its top reached
to heaven and was visible to the end of the whole earth, 21 whose
foliage was beautiful and its fruit abundant, and which provided
food for all, under which animals of the field lived, and in whose
branches the birds of the air had nests – 22 it is you, O king! You
have grown great and strong. Your greatness has increased and
reaches to heaven, and your sovereignty to the ends of the earth.
23 And whereas the king saw a holy watcher coming down from
heaven and saying, 'Cut down the tree and destroy it, but leave its
stump and roots in the ground, with a band of iron and bronze, in
the grass of the field; and let him be bathed with the dew of heaven,
and let his lot be with the animals of the field, until seven times pass
over him' – 24 this is the interpretation, O king, and it is a decree of
the Most High that has come upon my lord the king: 25 You shall be
driven away from human society, and your dwelling shall be with
the wild animals. You shall be made to eat grass like oxen, you shall
be bathed with the dew of heaven, and seven times shall pass over
you, until you have learned that the Most High has sovereignty
over the kingdom of mortals, and gives it to whom he will. 26 As it
was commanded to leave the stump and roots of the tree, your

kingdom shall be re-established for you from the time that you
learn that Heaven is sovereign. 27Therefore, O king, may my coun-
sel be acceptable to you: atone for your sins with righteousness, and
your iniquities with mercy to the oppressed, so that your prosperity
may be prolonged."

28All this came upon King Nebuchadnezzar. 29At the end of
twelve months he was walking on the roof of the royal palace of
Babylon, 30 and the king said, "Is this not magnificent Babylon,
which I have built as a royal capital by my mighty power and for
my glorious majesty?" 31While the words were still in the king's
mouth, a voice came from heaven: "O King Nebuchadnezzar, to
you it is declared: The kingdom has departed from you! 32You shall
be driven away from human society, and your dwelling shall be
with the animals of the field. You shall be made to eat grass like
oxen, and seven times shall pass over you, until you have learned
that the Most High has sovereignty over the kingdom of mortals
and gives it to whom he will." 33Immediately the sentence was fulfilled against Nebuchadnezzar. He was driven away from human
society, ate grass like oxen, and his body was bathed with the dew
of heaven, until his hair grew as long as eagles' feathers and his nails
became like birds' claws.

34When that period was over, I, Nebuchadnezzar, lifted my eyes
to heaven, and my reason returned to me.

I blessed the Most High,
    and praised and honored the one who lives forever.
For his sovereignty is an everlasting sovereignty,
    and his kingdom endures from generation to generation.
35All the inhabitants of the earth are accounted as nothing,
    and he does what he wills with the host of heaven
    and the inhabitants of the earth.
There is no one who can stay his hand or say to him,
    "What are you doing?"

36At that time my reason returned to me; and my majesty and
splendor were restored to me for the glory of my kingdom. My

counselors and my lords sought me out, I was re-established over
my kingdom, and still more greatness was added to me. 37Now I,
Nebuchadnezzar, praise and extol and honor the King of heaven,

for all his works are truth,
    and his ways are justice;
and he is able to bring low
    those who walk in pride.

Who Shall Perish, and Who Be Delivered

Daniel 3 and 4 How to take seriously the spectacular story recounted here of the youths in the fiery furnace? Let us regard it as of more import than, say, a tale told for the instruction of Sunday School children. (Perhaps we resolve the unsettling implications of the story by relegating it to youngsters, thus distancing, even trivializing it?)

The episode lies too close for comfort. Close indeed, and torrid. Scorching, a near memory of furnaces of our lifetime, stoked against the innocent. So we incline to put the image of the furnace at distance, as we do other horrors of the age: cluster bombs, land mines, smart missiles, napalm, rubber bullets; successive incursions, whether in Vietnam, Iraq, Panama, Grenada, or Central America.

The plain fact is that our nation, along with its nuclear cronies, is quite prepared to thrust enormous numbers of humans into furnaces fiercely stoked. Of the preparation and commission of such crimes, of their technique and strategic advantage, we have learned a great deal. But of repentance we have learned precisely nothing.

As a nation, nothing. As a church, perhaps something. It seems impossible to keep one's own story from dovetailing with the story of Daniel and his friends. Always some peaceable action brusquely summons those I love into the hot belly of the legal juggernaut!

As I first set down these notes, I girded myself for a journey to Syracuse (New York) to attend yet one more court appearance of my brother Jerry. His crime: he dared, in his stubborn way, to enter the Griffiths Air Force Base in Rome and to plead there for the children of the world. The action, it goes without saying, was not favorably received. The law concurs; his action was criminal.

The nuclear plague is of course legally protected. It is also self-engendered, deliberate, huckstered worldwide with a scientific sangfroid. Through the collusion of governments and scientists, the stoking of nuclear furnaces proceeds apace, at Griffiths as elsewhere. At that notorious base, surrounded by innocent fields and domestic animals, are stored tactical nuclear weapons in great numbers, destined (at the time) for export to Europe. From the same base at a later time, "nuclear capable" bombers were launched against Baghdad.

In the Syracuse courtroom (or in any other courtroom in the nation) no mention of international law will be tolerated. Nor will the so-called argument from necessity, in virtue of which violation of a law is permitted in order to prevent a greater evil. Nothing of these. The fact that provocative weapons of omni-destruction are lodged at Griffiths will not be in contention. Not even, so to speak, in mention.

Other topics will be explored. Arousing the prosecution to indignant rhetoric will be a minor infraction committed by a few fractious souls. Their crime is this – insisting, in whatever way is open to them (not many gates or hearts are open), that the existence of such places as Griffiths is morally appalling and tactically insane.

Meantime across our nation and world, research and deployment of such weapons continues. The fiery nuclear furnace is stoked to "seven times its heat." Despite momentous changes everywhere fomenting in the world, including many hopeful auguries of peace, the American race to oblivion proceeds.

That race has its own inner urge: ever more and more! It is as though a juggernaut has been launched downhill; it requires no other engine than its own massive momentum. It gathers speed apart from personality, political party, the second thoughts of the (few) thoughtful officeholders. It matters not a whit who inhabits the White House, who is appointed Chief of Staff, who sits in Congress or the Supreme Court; it matters not at all that former enemies have been quelled or overcome. The Bomb rules; together with its "conventional" relatives and progeny, it rules the economy, decrees who is to be enriched and who impoverished, and across the world, who is to live and who perish. The Bomb has even stolen a capital letter from the deity.

And we verify once more the central text of Paul: "Our battle is not against human forces, but against the principalities and powers, the rulers of this world of darkness, the evil spirits in regions above" (Eph. 6:12).

Daniel 3:1 ff. As to the golden image decreed by the king, it is absurdity upon caprice. The statue, we are informed straight-faced, is of enormous size. It is also badly, even hallucinatorially proportioned: "ninety feet by nine." Is there a conscious irony here? Does the royal pomposity not see how this form appears as the bizarre, larger-than-life sign of a demented self-regard, a morally grotesque ego?

It may fairly be taken, though left unmentioned, that the image operates on many levels. It is an image of a god otherwise unknown, not even named. It is also, as suggested above, an image of the king himself. (So also avers the first Christian commentator, Hippolytus.)

If the latter version holds, one may venture that the statue is erected to forestall the bad news implicit in the king's dream. The dream was unsettling in the extreme. So the disproportionate deific image attempts to offset the king's demise and the downfall of his kingdom as prophetically announced by Daniel. Also, one thinks, the colossus is concocted to forestall the advent of the final Realm, the rock that crushes and cancels in its wake every human intervention and polity.

Yet another aspect of the story: it is recounted to fortify and hearten a persecuted people. Let us be of good cheer: mock the oppressor, his pretensions to divine rank! In the eye of the beholder, the statue is rendered altogether ironic and banal. It is as though the image were despite all one of a surreal clown or a court fool.

The image in place, a command is issued. Let all and sundry fall before the statue to worship it! Time is collapsed; decree and obeisance are one. Daniel, tongue in cheek, catalogues "all peoples, nations, languages" obeying on the instant. No interval, no second thoughts, no recalcitrants (except for a few!). We are in a nightmarish world of automatons. Citizenship as an idol? Daniel's is a theology from below, with a vengeance.

The account is mimicry, incantation, caricature, deconstruction all. As though to say in code, "Note, please, the superabundant foolishness of this would be superhuman and his minions!" To this has come the empire, emperor and citizenry both, bound in a single bundle of banality. It is as though a colony of termites were at work, bringing down a shack, long gone in wrack and ruin. The royal pretensions are denied and derided in the very fact of reporting them.

The king's glory reaches to high heaven. He has achieved an astonishing world conquest (Dan. 3:4). What more attractive to the imperial djinn than a celebration of his empery – that his victories be fused into permanence through an overpowering and dizzying image?

In the eyes of Daniel something more than a rampageous royal ego is at work here. Through its image, the empire is rendered demonic. Which is to say, a powerful political, military, economic (religious?) entity is raised to proclaim absolute dominion over life and death.

We have here an event, the Bible suggests, that is a constant of imperial history. In a parallel passage in Revelation, an otherwise unnamed tyrant issues a summons similar to that of Nebuchadnezzar: worship the Beast, or perish (Rev. 5:9; 9:9; 13:7; 14:6; 17:15). A running thread binds one testament to another, and the behavior of an early empire with a later one. Are not all such entities genetically related? In attempting to seize the prerogatives of God, the empires are remarkably, lethally consistent. Or so the imagery and teaching would have us ponder.

Against these great odds the "faith of the saints" is called to steadfastness. Beware! Certain forms of fealty commanded by rulers are usurpations of the adoration due God alone. The godlings must be resisted, even at the price of capital execution.

In stark contrast to Daniel's community, all levels of dignity in the realm are promptly inducted into worship of the massive image. Rank and protocol are fastidiously observed, a charade of pomp, power, and prestige is mounted. The scene, reminiscent of later spectacles, is designed to bedazzle and stupefy and subdue, to bring to heel even mettlesome spirits. All are summoned.

The procession advances; it is as though the scribe were holding his breath in awe (or perhaps stifling with difficulty his derisive laughter): "princes, governors, lieutenant governors, commissioners, treasurers, judges, magistrates, and all other officials of the provinces."

The implied message is clear as a trumpet blast. A vast imperial bureaucracy has closed ranks; it is one in fealty. Of what avail, then, the resistance of a few diehards, were such to occur? And even more to the point, what god could bear comparison with this colossus? (Dan. 3:4–5) Thus the scene unfolds, meticulously described, a catalog of folly, a travesty of the honor due true merit.

A great huffing and puffing is underway. Need it be added that the votaries are unprepared for the hard tumble to follow?

Daniel 3:6–12 "You will prostrate yourselves and adore." (The appalling phrase is repeated word for word in Rev. 13:15). The high and mighty, along with the lowly and powerless, duly fall to ground. For Daniel and his community, the moment of truth approaches.

They are, by all indication, deliberately absent from the scene. The transgression is noted, and the resisters shortly denounced. The motive of the adversaries, one can judge, is envy (Dan 3:8). Feet have been stepped on, aspirants thrust to one side. And outsiders, exiles, of no account, have been granted high powers and prerogatives. And now, O king, behold the ultimate arrogance. The same beneficiaries have dared spurn your royal will! Thus God is placed in contention versus the gods. So also Daniel's understanding of faith is verified; a faithful community will inevitably be subject to crisis, and to the impending threat of the mighty.

We would much prefer to freeze in its remote time and place such idolatry as is described here, as though to think (and thus we often are prone to think), "Good riddance; we've done with all that." Yet the exact opposite is true. We moderns continue fervently to construct our own pantheon, gods violent, voracious, greedy. Ancient appetites, grievances, hostilities, jealousies arise, a fury of greed, envy, ego, hypothesized in a technological setting. Numerous shrines are consecrated to the gods of the nation, to the gods of manifest destiny, nuclear security, and so on.

Is the shrine of national idolatry the Pentagon, the Congress, the Supreme Court, the White House? Or perhaps all these in concert, with their vast paraphernalia of weaponry, their network of acolytes, diplomats, scientists, engineers, economists, sociologists, apologists? And yes, their enemies – hypothetical, virtual, nonexistent, the dark saturnalia of the imperial psyche?

And the silent churches, what of them? Where can worship of true God be found intact? As for ourselves – indifferent, silent, and politically enlisted – what judgment shall be leveled?

Judgment is already leveled. Imperial misbehavior reaches down and down, into a rapacious economy, political corruption, cruelties exacting more and more tribute. The crime awaits the "day of Jahweh." In Daniel and the prophets that day is anticipated, dramatized for our sober instruction.

In a twilit meantime the imperium proceeds to guard, venerate (and inevitably pay dearly) for the apparatus of what Archbishop Romero called the "security regime." Though he was referring to his own tormented country, El Salvador, his analysis has an eerie ring of truth for our situation as well:

> By virtue of this ideology, the individual is placed at the total service of the state. His or her political participation is suppressed...People are put into the hands of...elites, and are subjected to policies that oppress and repress all those who oppose them...The armed forces are put in charge of social and economic structures, under the pretext of the interests of national security. Everyone not at one with the state is declared a national enemy...The interests and advantages of the few are thus turned into an absolute. This absolute becomes a mystique. The national security regime thus attempts to give itself a good public image by a profession of Christian faith. So it presents itself as the only, or the best defender of the Christian civilization of the west. The omnipotence of these national security regimes, the total disregard they show toward individuals and

> their rights…turn national security into an idol. Like the god Moloch, the idol demands the daily sacrifice of many victims in its name. The term "security" is thus cruelly perverted. For in the name of national security, the insecurity of the individual becomes institutionalized.

It goes without saying that from the works and pomps of this political-military idol, God, the God of Daniel and Isaiah and Jeremiah and Jesus, is summarily excluded. Or if granted place, our deity is shunted to an out-of-the way alcove reserved for a minor potentate. And the worship goes on. Placation, imprecation, intercession, adoration. Moreover, the tribute is offered strictly on a *quid pro quo* basis. The god is required to produce, whether the benefit be a successful war or a booming economy.

Too, the shrine of the god is neatly situated; it lies just adjacent to the market place, each provenance greatly benefiting from the prospering of the other. Is not commerce in need of a blessing, and is not the temple graced by the shower of gold released in its direction by this Croesus?*

It is helpful to clarify the question raised by Daniel and his companions as they confront the gods of the kings. The question is not precisely "one god or many?" Rather, "true God or false?" That the true God is one, and the false gods many, is only a partial statement of the terms of conflict. Conceivably, the king could regard himself as a monotheist, but his (one) god, his monstrous image, could hardly be thought of as true God. The image is in fact closer in spirit to the beast of apocalypse.

Inevitably, belief in God raises questions of conduct, as Daniel and his friends well know. The king's behavior, his preposterous edicts tumbling out and out, unmask the base

*Croesus – Lydian king (d. 546 BCE) of legendary wealth.

quality of his faith. He remains ethically unhinged, cruel, overweening, bellicose. So degraded a spirit raises the towering image of a supreme god. And not at all strange, this god resembles the king.

Shall we raise here the vexed question of forced conversion (even to the "true faith")? It is striking, the contrast between the conduct of the king and that of the three youths, *vis à vis* their respective faiths. For his part, the king would tighten the screws: believe or die! The youths, on the other hand, have little to say, even as, under the slings and arrows of adversaries, they have much to endure. They utter nothing of threat or reproof, whether against their tormentor or his complaisant minions. What kind of witness is this? Is the God they worship true God? Are others invited to believe as they do?

They are a silent trio; they neither raise questions nor offer answers. They force no one's hand. Simply, the truth of their lives speaks for them: they are prepared to die for their belief. Enveloped in a mysterious silence, they offer their Torquemada* a true defense. In this exemplary moment they are thus commended to the generations, our own misadventurous one included. Their credential is a pure light in a dark time: nonviolent steadfastness.

Daniel 3:13 The king summons them, and the threat is repeated: Renounce your god, and embrace mine (i.e., me) – or die. For what conceivable god could deliver you from my hand? Your god, my god. A pantheon of idols shores up the king's theology. (See the derisory account of the Babylonian pantheon in Isaiah 44:9–17, 40:19–20, and 46:1–2.)

In this matter of the nature and number of the god (or

*Torquemada – the feared inquisitor of medieval fame.

gods), nothing is clear; the king's pate is a muddle. Does there exist one god, or a number of these? Two gods exist, if he is to embrace (even to a degree) the faith of Daniel; namely, the king's sacred image, and the god (sic) of the trio. And must it not follow that one god is inevitably pitted against another, in the manner of earthly tyrants locked in a war of supremacy?

Given the ethical demands of their faith, the three youths are easy targets of the enemy. The command of their God (Exod. 20:3–5; Deut. 5:7–9) is austere and leaves no room for accommodation. "No gods before me...no graven image... neither bow down nor serve them..."

God is able to deliver them, the youths insist. But the deliverance may or may not be granted, as they concede. Still, whether the outcome be good or ill is beside the point. At least beside their point, which is one of unflinching faith and trust. They state calmly the worst case (v. 18). Suppose they are not delivered; suppose they perish? Let it be known beforehand and stated clearly: they were condemned for refusing to worship the king's grotesquerie; for that they died. Thus nothing in the final statement of the resisters is to be construed as doubting God's power to save. They simply say: "Take our lives as it pleases You, or leave us our lives, intact. The outcome is in hands other than ours."

In such a world as Daniel's (or our own) God is presented (one thinks quite deliberately) as a kind of "worst case" – feeble, distant, incapacitated, set at naught by the great bulk and barrier of the idol. And our trio much resembles their God; they are entirely at the mercy of the earth-shaker and his brobdingnagian statue. In this too, powerless and vulnerable, they are admirable images of the God they serve. Counter images as well, of the overbearing implausible statue.

How, finally, is the story and its miraculous outcome to be

understood – especially by those who come on little evidence of a favorable outcome to other witnesses in equally bleak times? The bloody evidence of our century goes contrary to anything remotely suggesting success, as it is commonly and culturally peddled.

"Alas," and a great groaning from the guts; this is the cry of the noblest among us – the prisoners of conscience, the advocates, the victims. Has there been in all history such a woeful tumble and jumble of years as those of our lifetime? So many victims, so many have been seized, tortured, perished, disappeared, for the most part alone and unsuccored. *Ac si non esset Deus;** God is so nearly a nonentity, non-intervenor, non-savior that to make any claim of availability, love, and compassion – of providence overriding awful event – were to submit it to the derision of the powerful.

It comes to this, in the eye of many: God or no God, providence, chance, mischance – what difference? The world goes its implacable way, the virtuous perish, the wicked prosper. No hint of intervention from on high, no tit for tat, no reward for awesome (some would say obsessive) fidelity. Of what advantage then, the faith of the persecuted, the tortured, the disappeared?

A supposition. The *apologia* or defense of the youths (and of a multitude of heroic spirits before them, and after) cannot be understood in terms of advantage or reward – even in terms of deliverance. All such language is beside the point. It is closer to the king's superstition than to the spirit of the resisters.

It comes to this, a hard saying. Nothing of advantage, as the world would judge or weigh such, accrues to faith. Faith is no bargain struck in the market, no canny eye upon a main

* *Ac si non esset Deus* – "As if God did not exist."

chance. To say "I believe" is to hand over to life and death (that is, to the God of life and death) a blank check.

Faith. The scene is Ravensbruck, Germany, a notorious Nazi death camp for women. The characters, author Corrie ten Boom and her sister, Betsie, who have been deported there from Haarlem, Netherlands. Their crime? Concealing Jews in their home. Ten Boom remembers:

> Life in Ravensbruck took place on two separate levels, mutually impossible. One, the observable, external life, grew every day more horrible. The other, the life we lived with God, grew daily better, truth upon truth, glory upon glory. Sometimes I would slip the Bible from its little sack with hands that shook, so mysterious had it become to me. It was new; it had just been written. I marveled sometimes that the ink was dry. I had believed the Bible always, but reading it now had nothing to do with belief. It was simply a description of the way things were – of hell and heaven, of how people act and how God acts...

King and youths face to face; a powerful moment. And we remember another such scene: "You shall stand before magistrates and princes; and fret not as to what you shall say. The words will be given you in that hour." (Mark 13:11) As comes true.

Undoubtedly, as we learn from a prior crisis, the little knot of believers has been at prayer. Their response to the king's command is peremptory and to the point. If the God whom we worship is capable of delivering us...God will do so. But even if there is no deliverance, know that we still refuse to adore your image or serve your god. Nothing could be clearer. Or more liable to dire consequence.

Daniel 3:19–23 The king's will is spurned. His anger explodes. The furnace is stoked to seven times its usual conflagration; the three are securely bound. At all cost the king's god must prevail. Thus every precaution is taken, lest the God of the three refusers should intervene.

Daniel 3:24–30 Shortly thereafter the king approaches the furnace and peers in. Astounding! The youths are unharmed, unbound, treading the fires. And a mysterious fourth figure has joined them, one who wears the aspect of a "son of the gods," a guardian angel (Dan. 3:25). The faithful are not abandoned. An angel substitutes for the absent Daniel.

A curt regal order, and the fires are banked. The king is deeply moved by the miraculous intervention. Summoning the three as they issue from the torrid circle, he hails them as "servants of the most high God."

Thus once again the story embraces unlikelihood; the impossible comes to pass. The lesson? No one lies outside the swath of providence; even a criminal ruler may be saved. The God of the faithful ones has worked yet another wonder; the oppressor too is "delivered."

A catalog of attendant marvels follows. The officials of the court are summoned; they rub their eyes in wonderment. No least harm has come to the youths; their hair is unsinged, their clothing intact, and finally, "no odor of fire lingers about them." (Dan. 3:27) The king is in ecstasy, his praise of God exceeds all bounds.

A pentecost! Like the king of Nineveh in the days of Jonah (Jon. 3:6–9), this one has been utterly changed. And the youths, greater by far than Jonah, witness to the truth in silence and renunciation, at risk of their lives. They have seemingly wrought in the king conversion of heart, reversal of his awful former course. A king, a world conqueror, and now – a believer? He is delivered from his own hellish fires. (Dan. 3:28)

Thus the effect of heroic obedience is underscored. The

three, by the king's own word, trusting in God, have disobeyed the orders of the king, and have handed over their bodies, rather than serving or adoring a god other than true God. The episode marks the sole appearance in the book of the famous three resisters. But their place in biblical history is secure. Mattathias places them in a catalogue of the great spirits of Israel (1 Macc. 2:58–59). "Ananias, Azarias and Mishael believed and were saved from the fire."

The king, according to our storyteller, is an extremely complex character, much given to fits and starts of mood. Given also to dreaming and mulling, threatening, rewarding, loving, exacting revenge. A Saul, one thinks, a son of thick darkness and meager light. The imperial motto seems to be: "Turn, turn, turn." From idolatry to true worship, from fury to ample rewarding of former adversaries. He is, in sum, not greatly to be trusted. In service to him one may don the purple today and tomorrow cower beneath the executioner's ax.

Daniel and his friends walk this royal gauntlet of mood, frenzy, fidget, and frown. Remarkably, they survive; more, in the above episode and the one to follow, they exert on the king an effect utterly transforming. Heroic guides, experienced, wise beyond their years, they draw this tormented ruler through a knothole of ambition and pride, loss and suffering. Through and through – into freedom. He tastes a fate he had devised for others – and thought himself immune from. And finally he comes forth from darkness into a blaze of dawn, a difficult redemption.

Once more the focus shifts back to Daniel. All praise to him as he takes center stage, a rare, all but unique exemplar. He stands with his people in yet another crisis, even as he proceeds to challenge the powers. Once more he must act with adroitness, appear to play the king's game, to serve, bow and scrape. But only to a point.

The near point facing him, like the point of a sword, is a question of complicity or betrayal. He might well be impaled. So be it. Has he not vowed in his heart that come what may, the truth will be spoken?

Daniel 4:1 ff. As in Chapter 2, we are offered a royal dream. Here a less dangerous atmosphere prevails; no threats are uttered, no demands, stalling and appalling, are placed on the interpreters. Perhaps, one thinks, even kings grow reasonable.

The present dream is of a tree, the apotheosis of abundance. Our friend the king, now exorcised of the image that obsessed him, appears in a far different guise – and a more hopeful one. His dream is of something alive and flourishing.

What a tree! This one, like no plant sprung from earth, embraces and claims for its own earth and sky and sea. Its roots sink deep; its branches tower above, encompassing the horizon, and holding in their embrace all peoples, nations, living beings. (Dan. 4:10–12)

A pristine image, and an attractive one. Are we to think of the "other side" of empire – the neglected side, ignored in the awful proceedings of battlefield and council, betrayal and intrigue? The side, perhaps, that urges a ruler to act in morally ecological fashion, to cherish and be accountable to creation?

Alas, the dream proposes not only an ideal, it offers symbols also of a tragic shortfall. Suddenly this king, this seizer-Caesar of all things – of nations, and of the earth itself, and thereby of the future – this one is brought down as though he were the splendid tree, and Someone were wielding an ax against him. We could not be offered a more vivid image of the outcome of ungodly pride.

The occasion of the royal downfall is puzzling. The king paces about on his palace roof, reflecting with satisfaction on his own excellence and accomplishments. What more usual recreation than this? Thus do the great ones disport themselves. They lust after riches, honors, the credit of a name. These attained, they pace about tranquilly, decked in their laurels. And we grant them their musing frivolities with a sigh.

But God does not grant them. Nor in Greek myths or elsewhere do the gods grant them. Prometheus steals fire; Oedipus transgresses laws of nature. And suddenly their hubris brings them to naught. A warning is implicit here: even the close-woven communality of the human, its symbols buried deep in the lore of the tribe, can fray and fall apart, and ruin follow close.

We note here a rather consistent biblical image as well. Mysteriously (though not without warning, even if unheeded), the splendid imperium falls to pieces. Top-heavy with the grandiose pretensions of bureaucracy and privilege, blind if not contemptuous toward the suffering inflicted by force and devious diplomacy and piratical economics – the splendid heaven-reaching colossus cracks and falls.

Few, it seems, read "the signs of the times" commended to us by scripture. On the contrary, almost everyone pays heed, even fealty, to the "signs of empire," to proclamations of prosperity, of the sound estate of polity, of security intact, of the purportedly selfless virtuousness of authorities and the malfeasance of enemies. Signs that are utterly deceptive.

Attending to such, or trusting them, spells a ruinous simple-mindedness. Yet many attend; many trust. In consequence few are prepared for outcomes and revelation, for Watergates, contra "concealments," perfidies such as those that propelled Gulf War slaughter – for the stunning greed of a CIA-funded drug culture. Kings and counselors, everyone (except for a few visionaries invariably dismissed as fools) is set off balance. Pride and despair meet and meld in a common folly.

In our story the social catastrophe is concentrated in singular images: the fate of the tree, the fate of the king (Dan. 4:13–14). The splendid tree, we are told, crashes down. And with its fall, all that dwelt in its web of life, nested in it, fed from it, clung to its boughs, sought the horizon at its summit, took refuge and refreshment there – all are put to flight or to death. Misuse has issued in disuse. And finally, in disaster.

So the king falls, and everything around him lies in shambles. A Lear, he is fated to play out a centrifugal drama of power and pride. Here, as in the Revelation sequence, an angel pronounces sentence. The words of the angel are terrible (Dan 4:15–17). Judgment falls; it is as though the skies fell. Unhouseled,* senseless as a beast of the fields, the king will wander the earth, till "seven times pass over him," the period of his purgation.

How the mighty are fallen – kingly tree and king! The outcome is replete with terror and irony; the physical degradation of the ruler embodies and dramatizes his moral estate. He set his throne on high. From there, dominating and decreeing, he proceeded to play god in matters of life and death. "To the furnace...To the lions' den!" And murder being the "final solution" to one of his habits, he passed capital sentence even on a friend.

Never, it goes without saying, in his worst and wildest dream, is his own conduct scrutinized or sentence passed on himself. But now, in broad daylight, sentence is passed on him. Not a capital one, but a purgative one; for God is a God of mercy, even to the merciless.

So there is hope for both tree and king. The angel of Daniel announces, after the worst, a kind of hopeless hope. The stump of the tree will stand, humiliated and stripped;

*Unhouseled – not having received the Eucharist, and thus not consecrated.

but alive for all that, eventually to send forth hardy shoots.

We could not have a more vivid image of the cross, crudely carpentered from a tree that once burgeoned with life and rejoiced in it. This tree, for all its passionate beauty, was abused the more. The lofty, noble being was reduced to dead planks conjoined. Now nothing is left to be destroyed except the One who clings there.

Thus the meaning Daniel attaches to the dream is not merely the end of an empire; such a theme is no more than a biblical commonplace. The destruction is, after all, but a turn of the wheel of crime and accountability.

We are advised by the dream that something of far greater import is at stake. Christ crucified is the prelude of the realm of God. The splendid tree of creation, twisted like a bonsai, tormented into the form of tree of empire, must be stripped before it can be healed, before it can lay claim once more to its capacity, its fruits, life, amplitude, wholeness, can welcome song, community, sweetness – before it can come to rebirth. The tree of creation is transformed and becomes the tree of the Realm of God. But not yet.

First there is loss. Like the angel of Revelation (Rev. 18), we must chant a threnody for that beauty, that promise come to naught. Let us ponder it: crime – socialized, unaccountable, specious, and beguiling – will eventually be brought to account.

And then, and then? At the dead end of false hope, an act of God may bring on something new, something unprecedented, beyond human longing. Something before whose advent we are powerless as the dead – powerless to impede, powerless as well to bring about.

The Writing on the Wall

The Book of Daniel

5 King Belshazzar made a great festival for a thousand of his
lords, and was drinking wine in the presence of the thousand.
[2]Under the influence of the wine, Belshazzar commanded that
they bring in the vessels of gold and silver that his father Nebuchadnezzar had taken out of the temple in Jerusalem, so that the
king and his lords, his wives, and his concubines might drink from
them. [3]So they brought in the vessels of gold and silver that had
been taken out of the temple, the house of God in Jerusalem, and
the king and his lords, his wives, and his concubines drank from
them. [4]They drank the wine and praised the gods of gold and silver, bronze, iron, wood, and stone.

[5]Immediately the fingers of a human hand appeared and began
writing on the plaster of the wall of the royal palace, next to the
lampstand. The king was watching the hand as it wrote. [6]Then the
king's face turned pale, and his thoughts terrified him. His limbs
gave way, and his knees knocked together. [7]The king cried aloud to
bring in the enchanters, the Chaldeans, and the diviners; and the
king said to the wise men of Babylon, "Whoever can read this writing and tell me its interpretation shall be clothed in purple, have a
chain of gold around his neck, and rank third in the kingdom."
[8]Then all the king's wise men came in, but they could not read the
writing or tell the king the interpretation. [9]Then King Belshazzar
became greatly terrified and his face turned pale, and his lords were
perplexed.

[10]The queen, when she heard the discussion of the king and his
lords, came into the banqueting hall. The queen said, "O king, live
forever! Do not let your thoughts terrify you or your face grow pale.
[11]There is a man in your kingdom who is endowed with a spirit of
the holy gods. In the days of your father he was found to have enlightenment, understanding, and wisdom like the wisdom of the
gods. Your father, King Nebuchadnezzar, made him chief of the
magicians, enchanters, Chaldeans, and diviners, [12]because an excellent spirit, knowledge, and understanding to interpret dreams, ex-

plain riddles, and solve problems were found in this Daniel, whom the king named Belteshazzar. Now let Daniel be called, and he will give the interpretation."

[13]Then Daniel was brought in before the king. The king said to Daniel, "So you are Daniel, one of the exiles of Judah, whom my father the king brought from Judah? [14]I have heard of you that a spirit of the gods is in you, and that enlightenment, understanding, and excellent wisdom are found in you. [15]Now the wise men, the enchanters, have been brought in before me to read this writing and tell me its interpretation, but they were not able to give the interpretation of the matter. [16]But I have heard that you can give interpretations and solve problems. Now if you are able to read the writing and tell me its interpretation, you shall be clothed in purple, have a chain of gold around your neck, and rank third in the kingdom."

[17]Then Daniel answered in the presence of the king, "Let your gifts be for yourself, or give your rewards to someone else! Nevertheless I will read the writing to the king and let him know the interpretation. [18]O king, the Most High God gave your father Nebuchadnezzar kingship, greatness, glory, and majesty. [19]And because of the greatness that he gave him, all peoples, nations, and languages trembled and feared before him. He killed those he wanted to kill, kept alive those he wanted to keep alive, honored those he wanted to honor, and degraded those he wanted to degrade. [20]But when his heart was lifted up and his spirit was hardened so that he acted proudly, he was deposed from his kingly throne, and his glory was stripped from him. [21]He was driven from human society, and his mind was made like that of an animal. His dwelling was with the wild asses, he was fed grass like oxen, and his body was bathed with the dew of heaven, until he learned that the Most High God has sovereignty over the kingdom of mortals, and sets over it whomever he will. [22]And you, Belshazzar his son, have not humbled your heart, even though you knew all this! [23]You have exalted yourself against the Lord of heaven! The vessels of his temple have been brought in before you, and you and your lords,

your wives and your concubines have been drinking wine from them. You have praised the gods of silver and gold, of bronze, iron, wood, and stone, which do not see or hear or know; but the God in whose power is your very breath, and to whom belong all your ways, you have not honored.

24"So from his presence the hand was sent and this writing was
inscribed. 25And this is the writing that was inscribed: *mene, mene,*
tekel, and *parsin.* 26This is the interpretation of the matter: *mene,*
God has numbered the days of your kingdom and brought it to an
end; 27*tekel,* you have been weighed on the scales and found wanting; 28*peres,* your kingdom is divided and given to the Medes and
Persians."

29Then Belshazzar gave the command, and Daniel was clothed in purple, a chain of gold was put around his neck, and a proclamation was made concerning him that he should rank third in the kingdom.

30That very night Belshazzar, the Chaldean king, was killed.
31And Darius the Mede received the kingdom, being about sixty-
two years old.

The Writing on the Wall

Daniel 5 The stage is set. Once more Daniel is to intervene and interpret an act of God. A larger implication is present, in this story as in the preceding. The one who "keeps the faith" is enabled to cast a canny eye on the ways of the world, in this case on pretentious imperial dreams. The others, the tyrants and their sycophants, are left helpless, dismayed, obsessed. It is a great theme, one arguably central to the Bible: the tumble of worldly expectations, salvation from "beneath."

Theater of the absurd? Perhaps, but with a deadly serious subplot. At stake is the survival of the heroic few and their compatriots, the enslaved community. The battle rages in the minds of victor and vanquished alike. Shall the tyrant win the absurd fealty he demands, thereby pulverizing the spirit of the exiles, even as he inflates himself like a regal blowfish? Mockery, deflation, mime, mimicry – great tools of survival, as we have seen before; the humor of the oppressed.

The fantasies of the powerful are acted out. This is a mortal danger to many; the would be omnipotents seduce, frighten, and destroy. Their emulation of the gods issues in a far-reaching folly. The work of truth-telling, courage, insight must intervene. Let the saving remnant stand firm, those at the bottom, those beyond the pale. These are a favorite biblical geography, and a blessed one, all told. Those who stand and suffer there become, with regard to their persecutors, an only hope.

Daniel 5:1–6 We are in a far different setting than the preceding dream sequence, or the autoidolatry of the great statue. We are informed that the son of Nebechudnezzar, King Belshazzar, has succeeded to the throne. Him, too, Daniel must counter. Like father, like son; the new king is as volatile and folly ridden as the former; he admits to no moral limits.

Our scene is a banquet hall with a vile celebration in progress. (We are told nothing concerning the occasion.) The plunder of the temple of Jerusalem is brought into the room. Misuse of the holy vessels is the intention, yet another crime of his sodden majesty. But there is more. Deliberately and with malicious forethought, the chalices and plates become instruments of idolatry. Belshazzar and his drunken crew lift a cup to the "gods of gold and silver, bronze, iron, wood, and stone" (Dan. 5:3–4).

We are thus offered another parabolic scene of sin in high places; here, gestures of contempt, blasphemous misuse of holy artifacts. Let it be noted that the obscene ritual is reproduced in other times and places. Today, too, gods of iron are hailed and celebrated as the saviors of humankind. And as modern monarchs pay tribute to nuclear gods of death in a similar scenario of ruin, they proceed also to pollute the creation.

It is all the same. One thinks of farmlands in the American Midwest, violated with nuclear bunkers. Of hundreds of thousands of citizen-churchgoers, favored, educated, and inducted into the sorry business of war and weaponry. Of the interlocking interests of government and church, each in its dim and delighted way pursuing common cause, blessing and seeking blessing. One principality hell bent and armed to the teeth, another morally muddled, as was clear in so many places during the Gulf slaughter. Twin follies. Yellow ribbons decking church buildings, even altars and tabernacles and pulpits. All unconsciously recalling (and reversing!) the image of Exodus, the lambs' blood staining the lintel of those to be spared. The ribbons signifying: we approve; more, we urge. Let war be taken to its logical end. Let the enemy perish.

One priest tells of his shock on entering a sanctuary where he found the tabernacle draped in an American flag. He removed the flag and for this was summarily evicted by the pastor.

The king's orgy is underway. Cups are lifted, obscene tributes paid. Then comes an interruption, an event more terrible than the epiphany of a ghost. Truth, reality – what to name it? This is no troubling dream. In broad daylight a hand appears, writing on the wall. Presumably the entire court witnesses the terror. Along with the ruler, his cohorts are shortly driven out of their vaporous wits. The preternatural hand is undeterred, literate. And it writes.

The revelers grow illiterate on the moment. What language is this, what message? Fear and trembling seize on all.

The impenetrable writing on the wall is one of the best known and most often invoked images in the Bible. How many tyrants have seen (and not seen) – as judgment is spelled out in a script of utmost scorn – a hand that declares their majesties redundant, swept into the dustbin of history!

Up to this moment the palace wall has been blank as the conscience of the king. Crime, consequence? Of these, a *tabula rasa.* Suddenly, with no warning, the hand appears, the message is inscribed, bold and clear. A greater power has descended upon the princely hall, marking it like a scroll of judgment with the inscrutable graffito.

Nothing of the message touches this royal illiterate. He is plagued with superstition; his limbs turn to water. There is something ludicrous in the dismay and confusion of a lord of the earth. Mouth agape, he blinks and peers about. On the moment he is stone sober.

The wall blazes. It is transformed; it becomes the page of a vast tome, a Bible crimsoned with blood. It is as though it bears the diatribe of a murdered prophet, this wall that proclaims a king's fearful fate. He cannot grasp it, we are told. Neither can his sycophantic clan, the foolish wise ones, always close at hand.

What can the words mean? Tongues buzz, heads shake. No more than the king can the counselors translate. The assembly is stalled, powerless. Equal benefits, equal ignorance.

Daniel 5:7–16 The story gathers tension. Who shall read the text aright? Extravagant rewards are held out. But hands drop, helpless; they cannot.

Thus is dramatized once more the biblical attitude toward the powers of this world, a reaction common to Daniel and other prophets as well. Profound scepticism, even derision. Behold these rulers and their entourage! A few bestride the world, many court favor, hearkening to royal pronouncements as though these were an epiphany of ineffable truths. Whoremongers and intellectual whores – together these create a mini-pantheon of folly.

Kings, take warning! The resisters are sane and clear eyed. And the kings? The likes of Nebechednezzar and Belshazzar are fools – self-created, self-deceived godlings.

We humans dwell in a world where mistakes befall (and are only now and then repaired), where good starts are frequently botched, and life wears for the most part an untidy, sorrowful, uncomprehending look. In such a world, claims of infallibility, superior wisdom, moral impeccability and the like are simply absurd, an illusion woven by the powerful – invariably to further their own ends.

The message of Daniel goes counter, and then some, by implication; let us view omnipotent or omniscient absurdities askance. And now and again, let us make mockery of the pronunciamentos of the powerful!

A preternatural *tour de force,* all said. The hand inscribes the great wall; the words are macaronic, combustible. And no one can interpret. In the breach, we note (the Bible notes) yet another overcoming of expectation, of conventional wisdom. Royal claims of moral clairvoyance are revealed for what they are: empty, void. The claimants are powerless. They can only blink and bray. The revelation, its terror (and yes, its hope) must await an outsider.

Once more, a breakthrough. Enter the queen. The disgraceful banquet seems to have been strictly a stag party; she was not a guest. Yet her absence is to her (and our) advantage. How rare a figure in that addled scene; how clear she is of head and heart! On her recommendation, amid the morbid dismay and incoherence, Daniel is summoned. Once more he stands at center stage, a protagonist of history. His life, his prayer, his companions (though absent from this episode) – these are his resource, his public credentials as well.

We take close note of his demeanor. He is modest, literate, and above all bold. What has he to lose in any case, since he desires nothing of the tawdry emoluments of the king?

He stands surrogate for a noble community. In centuries to come it will be known as "church" or "synagogue." True to his example, believers will announce again and again, before kings and judges and executioners, the meaning of the ominous message on the wall. The hand will never cease its writing, the text will never be expunged as long as authority persists in insulting and grisly ways.

Daniel 5:17–21 Without delay Daniel proceeds to decode the mysterious words. More risky by far, he dares improvise a coda on the words, taking the role of an Amos or a Jeremiah. Denunciation, then annunciation.

Daniel opens old wounds – he speaks of pride, the king's ancestral sin. An ominous start, and a necessary one. He begins, "a Daniel come to judgment." Dangerous, crucial, the memories! O king, as to your father, he exceeded every boundary of the human, every taboo. So he was condemned. He dwelt for punishment among beasts of the field, a beast among his kind.

And you, the son? You must learn the truth, even at this late hour. In this infernal banquet hall you repeat, indeed multiply former crimes. You dare steal the holy chalices and raise them to the honor of your gods.

Daniel 5:22–31 The exordium is a fearful one. (We note that it is gratuitously offered, of the prophet's own devising). If the king has forgotten, Daniel has not. The daring! "You, Belshazzar, have not humbled your heart, though you knew all this; you have exalted yourself against the Lord of heaven. The vessels of God's house you have brought in, and you (and yours) have drunk from them. And you have praised the gods of silver and gold, of bronze, iron, wood and stone, which do not see or hear or know. But the God in whose hand is your breath, and from whom all your ways take start, you have not honored" (Dan. 5:22–23). It is this God "in whose hand is your breath" – "by Him were the wrist and hand sent, and the writing set down" (Dan. 5:24). The sins of the father, ignored, indeed gloried in, are repeated by the son. Punishment is to be inevitable and swift.

Daniel now turns his attention to the wall and its text. *Mene mene:* "The days of the king are numbered, finished." *Tekel:* "He is weighed and found wanting." *Parsin:* "His kingdom is divided, given over." The misuse of the holy vessels is thus a symbol of a larger crime – of apostasy, rejection of God. "True to the message of the book of Daniel, time runs out for every empire of human creation."*

Including the American? Something more is at stake here than a theory concerning the rise and fall of imperial states. Something more than a catastrophe at hand, an outcome rendered inevitable by folly, greed and violence. Something more even than the consequence of high crime, a judgment countering the presumption that the high and mighty stand outside the law of God.

Does the biblical evidence come to this: that every empire is guilty of the sin of Belshazzar, and thereby falls from grace and eminence? That every empire pays obeisance to "gods of silver and gold, of bronze, iron, wood and stone, which do not see or hear or know?" The Word of God is hardly equivocal. In the banquet scene we touch on a truth, universal and in equal parts unpalatable: empires are by their very nature idolatrous. Their crimes dishonor the God of justice and peace. Their rulers wage stupendous wars, lay waste, pillage and defraud and crush the poor, claim life-and-death power in the world. History admits to no exceptions.

The judgment of Daniel is laid against the king's father (and by strong implication, upon the incumbent as well). It might serve as the epitaph of every such ruler in history: "Whom he

*Robert A. Anderson, *Signs and Wonders.*

would he slew, and whom he would he kept alive" (Dan. 5:19). The sin of the imperial one is generational – the sin known elsewhere as "original," a sin of origins, generationally renewed.

American idolatry? The gods of silver and gold are honored in greed and pillaging. The gods of bronze and iron are fashioned and paid fealty to in the workplaces of Mars, the god of war – in laboratories from Livermore, California, to Riverside, New York, where the ideology of empire is translated in ever more fearsome weaponry. The gods of wood and stone stand in our public spaces, icons raised in dubious honor of robber barons and warriors. Only connect! American history and geography is a vast diorama of idolatry in action.

And hand in hand with idolatry, worship that talks a like talk, walks the same walk. Judgment, standing counter, a word of truth? Rare indeed. And the worshipful, too – we ourselves – shall be judged.

Daniel and the Two Decrees

The Book of Daniel

6 It pleased Darius to set over the kingdom one hundred twenty
satraps, stationed throughout the whole kingdom, [2]and over
them three presidents, including Daniel; to these the satraps gave
account, so that the king might suffer no loss. [3]Soon Daniel distin-
guished himself above all the other presidents and satraps because
an excellent spirit was in him, and the king planned to appoint him
over the whole kingdom. [4]So the presidents and the satraps tried to
find grounds for complaint against Daniel in connection with the
kingdom. But they could find no grounds for complaint or any
corruption, because he was faithful, and no negligence or corruption could be found in him. [5]The men said, "We shall not find any
ground for complaint against this Daniel unless we find it in connection with the law of his God."

[6]So the presidents and satraps conspired and came to the king
and said to him, "O King Darius, live forever! [7]All the presidents of
the kingdom, the prefects and the satraps, the counselors and the
governors are agreed that the king should establish an ordinance
and enforce an interdict, that whoever prays to anyone, divine or
human, for thirty days, except to you, O king, shall be thrown into
a den of lions. [8]Now, O king, establish the interdict and sign the
document, so that it cannot be changed, according to the law of the
Medes and the Persians, which cannot be revoked." [9]Therefore
King Darius signed the document and interdict.

[10]Although Daniel knew that the document had been signed, he
continued to go to his house, which had windows in its upper
room open toward Jerusalem, and to get down on his knees three
times a day to pray to his God and praise him, just as he had done
previously. [11]The conspirators came and found Daniel praying and
seeking mercy before his God. [12]Then they approached the king
and said concerning the interdict, "O king! Did you not sign an
interdict, that anyone who prays to anyone, divine or human,
within thirty days except to you, O king, shall be thrown into a den
of lions?" The king answered, "The thing stands fast, according to

the law of the Medes and Persians, which cannot be revoked."
13Then they responded to the king, "Daniel, one of the exiles from
Judah, pays no attention to you, O king, or to the interdict you
have signed, but he is saying his prayers three times a day."

14When the king heard the charge, he was very much distressed.
He was determined to save Daniel, and until the sun went down he
made every effort to rescue him. 15Then the conspirators came to
the king and said to him, "Know, O king, that it is a law of the
Medes and Persians that no interdict or ordinance that the king
establishes can be changed."

16Then the king gave the command, and Daniel was brought
and thrown into the den of lions. The king said to Daniel, "May
your God, whom you faithfully serve, deliver you!" 17A stone was
brought and laid on the mouth of the den, and the king sealed it
with his own signet and with the signet of his lords, so that nothing
might be changed concerning Daniel. 18Then the king went to his
palace and spent the night fasting; no food was brought to him,
and sleep fled from him.

19Then, at break of day, the king got up and hurried to the den of
lions. 20When he came near the den where Daniel was, he cried out
anxiously to Daniel, "O Daniel, servant of the living God, has your
God whom you faithfully serve been able to deliver you from the
lions?" 21Daniel then said to the king, "O king, live forever! 22My
God sent his angel and shut the lions' mouths so that they would
not hurt me, because I was found blameless before him; and also
before you, O king, I have done no wrong." 23Then the king was
exceedingly glad and commanded that Daniel be taken up out of
the den. So Daniel was taken up out of the den, and no kind of
harm was found on him, because he had trusted in his God. 24The
king gave a command, and those who had accused Daniel were
brought and thrown into the den of lions – they, their children,
and their wives. Before they reached the bottom of the den the lions overpowered them and broke all their bones in pieces.

25Then King Darius wrote to all peoples and nations of every
language throughout the whole world: "May you have abundant

prosperity! 26I make a decree, that in all my royal dominion people should tremble and fear before the God of Daniel:

For he is the living God,
  enduring forever.
His kingdom shall never be destroyed,
  and his dominion has no end.
27He delivers and rescues,
  he works signs and wonders in heaven and on earth;
  for he has saved Daniel from the power of the lions."

28So this Daniel prospered during the reign of Darius and the reign of Cyrus the Persian.

Daniel and the Two Decrees

Daniel 6:1–5 Daniel's eminence in the kingdom continues under Darius the Mede. An extraordinary truth is once more clarified; providence is extended not only to the exiles, but to their oppressors and keepers as well. In a different way, of course. Indeed, how could God be thought provident toward the people of faith, were the Deity not vigilant also over the conduct, so often exploitative and murderous, of the nations? These will bear close watching, mitigating, taming, if the remnant is to survive. To this day, and on to the "end time" dear to Daniel's prophecy, such matters remain profoundly mysterious, and often as not, sanguinary.

It might not be redundant to recall again a central teaching of our book, touching on the providence of Jahweh. On occasion, and for a time only, and even then rarely, the just are protected from suffering and death at the hands of a brigand authority. But the happy outcome is hardly to be taken as a generalized message, whether we turn to the Hebrew bible or our own. In this matter, the fate of the prophets as well as the capital punishment of Jesus must be taken in account. For as such narratives proceed to their awful endings, we are offered all but an "Anti-Book of Daniel." As in the outcry of Jesus from the cross, God "forsakes" the anguished, dying one.

Thus in Daniel's story, a somber midrash of God lurks. To mortal Daniel, a bright "yes." To mortal Jesus, a "no," a turning away. As the earlier story is realized in Jesus, the future is shot with darkness. And for us – lo! the story of Daniel strikes free of the magic and idolatry of imperial courts, then and now. And we find ourselves delivered over to the Mystery.

Among the nations, the gods are made of silver and gold, bronze and iron, wood and stone. They are subsumed, all but submerged in the cosmology. The prevailing image of creation is a huge complex engine, requiring (on the part of authorities) vigilance and, on occasion, repair. Like the vitals of a town clock, it must be periodically oiled, adjusted, repaired. So preternatural interventions abound, votaries are plucked from death, worldly prosperity is conferred or denied. And the kings, whatever their moral stripe, are free in their time and place to mimic the gods. Godlings. For a time, in a space, they may play their games, superhuman and silly.

But to speak of the community of faith, and of Daniel, no such idiotic theodicy exists. Rather than wanton power, a far greater gift is implied and conferred; it is called hope. An unambiguous gift. A hope which includes the possibility of violent death, prison, torture, exile, persecution of every kind. A hope which, on a warranty and promise, and against all odds and evidence, hopes on – for reasons which surpass all reason.

Daniel's larger community, it will be remembered, is composed of radical outsiders, exiles, slave laborers. And we have seen a redemption of sorts, and stood in awe, not knowing what was to come of this. Daniel is summoned apart, he becomes a pristine insider. In face of harsh obstacles, hostility, intrigue and betrayal, he "makes it." We have seen, too, how dangerous is his new eminence, morally queasy, both enticing and forbidding.

Daniel proves incorruptable. To this degree, questions arise. Is he credible, we ask, this Himalayan eminence? Did he never once falter or totter, let alone fall? To our fault-ridden lives, he seems so inhumanly perfect! Still. Is the issue here Daniel's credibility? Given the awful situation of his people, is not Daniel-as-icon a necessary creation, crucial to the common survival – a figure necessarily drawn larger than life, his moral stature unmarred by weakness or mischance? It may be that in view of grave popular needs, the dark side of a hero must be protected from scrutiny. Faults, defects, moral weakness – out of sight, out of mind – at least for the duration of hard times!

Meantime we of another time and place have other questions to raise; other needs, a far different sensibility in fact. The meager times have made of us creatures of lowered expectations. And they are great times, in consequence, for digging in the landfill of human clay, seeking clues as to the less than admirable side of this or that hero. Are we in search, perhaps, of an anti-hero?

Again and again, consistent and unwavering, Daniel is shown at prayer (v. 10), and we are invited to take this seriously. The example is a clear offering to believers of any age, and requires no elaboration.

Daniel 6:6–11 Daniel continues to flourish. The envious take to poking about in his affairs and repute. They seek ways and means of bringing him to ruin. Dark consequences gather. Finding him to their discomfiture morally free of blemish, they adopt another tack. His religious discipline offers an opening: an edict of the king has forbidden all trafficking with divinities other than himself.

So Daniel is discovered at forbidden prayer, daring to address not the king, but Jahweh. The sycophants, inflated with their damning information, hasten to the king. And one wonders: could there exist on any throne known to history so gullible a ruler? The proposition of the mischief makers is an artful tribute to royal vanity. Like lampreys on a prey, their machinations fasten on his ego.

The king's ear is theirs. He combusts (or at least inflates) spontaneously. It is not immediately evident that he wishes to proclaim himself a god. Nonetheless, what a foolish edict!

"No one is to address a petition to god or man for thirty days, except to you, O King." Thirty days. And after that? The pronunciamento seems deliberately temporary, a kind of loyalty test, a pledge of allegiance. We recognize the ploy; it is perennially dear to the hearts of tyrants.

For a period of time, so the order has it, all petitions of whatever sort, religious or secular in scope, are to be addressed solely to himself. Thirty days. So be it. The clocks tick away, a countdown. Is this majesty bent on inducing a crisis, a final winnowing of grain from chaff? Eccentric as an insect buzzing about the palace, the monarch lands – naïve, earthbound, presumptuous, and suggestible – in the web woven by his conspirators.

About Daniel, in contrast, there hovers a sense of calm and self possession. He has confronted kings before, their folly and foibles. There is nothing for it; he goes about his routine as usual, as though under a noon sun, and no clouds gathering. Walking abroad he learns of the new decree and speedily returns home. There in an upper room he undertakes as usual his petitions (now capitally forbidden) to his God.

Let us pause to take in the scene. For Jews of the diaspora and exile, prayer spells freedom from the hellish wheel of Ixion.* The hours set aside for daily prayer represent a crucial interruption and relief, morning, afternoon, and evening. Prayer is a sign, a promise, time – even for the enslaved – that offers dignity and meaning, and outcome as well. We shall overcome.

Turning to prayer, Daniel utterly ignores the king and his ineffably foolish edict, as if to say, "Let us lead the lives we are summoned to; the rest is as dust." Did he conclude that an

*The wheel of Ixion – in Greek mythology, a burning wheel of punishment that rolls through the underworld.

approach to His Majesty was useless? In any case, he walks to a different drummer. He has a summons to answer, issued by his God. Prayer comes first. All other means and methods toward survival he holds in abeyance.

Daniel at prayer, Daniel courting danger. The scene will be repeated often in ensuing centuries. Inspiring to generations of latter-day saints and martyrs, this single-minded resolve invites long reflection, emulation, and gratitude.

Without delay the pursuants are at the door and burst in. Were the believers reverently silent, or chanting aloud? We know only that they were presumably turned toward the east, to Jerusalem, some five hundred miles distant.

The king's law is precise. One need only be taken *in delicto flagranti,* in the forbidden act of petitioning an outlawed God, to be swiftly undone.

As for ourselves, there is more than the plight of Daniel to consider at this juncture. There is another question – that of the exiled God. Willy nilly, the decrees that would crush the people also outlaw their deity. Thus according to the implied dramatic of the story, God has embraced the humiliated estate of the people of God.

The congruence between the criminalized believer and the forbidden God is striking, though by no means historically unique. Recall the slaughter in the Iraqi desert, a terrifying instance. As bombs fell, one could only declare that the first casualty of the war was Jesus, his teaching and example. Outlawed "for the duration." In place of an unequivocal instruction concerning love of enemies, we were presented with a witless verbal charade caparisoned in religious garb. To wit, something known as the "just war theory." Something followed by indiscriminate, unaccountable mass murder.

In fact, the war "won" for us Americans and our warriors a pyhrric victory. The killing of the innocent continues to this day in a war of sanctions. But literally nothing of our benighted objectives of war has been reached. A tyrant continues in office. Children continue to die. And to speak of American soldiers, multitudes are mysteriously fallen ill. Were they exposed to nuclear fallout? The Pentagon has conveniently lost the documentation that might shed light on their malady. And what of the just war theory? Once again a supremely unjust war puts the theory to naught. As well as the theorists.

Speaking with perspicacity of the fall of the Roman empire, Thomas Cahill writes:

> There are no doubt lessons here for the contemporary reader... The creation of an increasingly unwieldy and rigid bureaucracy, whose own survival becomes its overriding goal...the lip service paid to values long dead; the pretense that we still are what we once were; the increasing concentration of the populace into richer and poorer by way of a corrupt tax system, and the desperation that inevitably follows; the aggrandizement of executive power at the expense of the legislature; ineffectual legislation promulgated with great show; the moral vocation of the man at the top to maintain order at all costs, while growing blind to the cruel dilemmas of ordinary life – these are all themes with which our world is familiar, nor are they the God-given property of any party or political point of view, though we often act as though they were.

Little can be done to counter the royal decree, but that little is done. It proves crucial, and not only to Daniel and his companions. When the community falls to prayer, the act does not seem to be a last-ditch recourse of beleaguered victims. Nothing appears frantic or hasty or improvised. It is simply the accustomed order of the day, a liturgy to be observed, be the times prosperous or ill. Shall there be, on the day of testing, any variation in holy routine? By no means.

Daniel 6:12–13 The churls burst in, seize Daniel and hustle him off to the king. It brings to mind a later scene. Another Accused stands before a judge. And the renowned Defendant speaks not a word. His crime has been fabricated by guileful enemies, the outcome long ago arranged. Of what point, then, words? Jesus is silent (Matt. 27:12–14).

"God is my judge" (Dan. 6:14). What to do? The king gnaws his fingers; he is hoisted on his own legal petard. It is not the first occasion, nor the last, when the law wears a two-edged look. It turns with lethal intent against the innocent. At the same time, it trips up the eminence who has sworn to abide by the law, come hell or high water – come, more to the point, intrusion of a higher law.

Hell is kindled to a firestorm when otherwise good men pronounce such oaths as, Yes, I will fervently and equably wield the sword of the law. (No need to speak of the catastrophe when wicked men, or weak men, swear a like oath.) We speak here, alas, of the majority of judges today.

At the swearing in of judges (a curious symbolic act) a cliché comes forcibly to mind: "Justice is blind." The saying is often intoned on such occasions. It is commonly regarded as a veritable Sinaitic dictum, implying that a wisdom descended from on high now rests upon the candidate, a wisdom beyond human challenge. It is conventionally translated as something like this: justice is impartial; it takes no account of accidents of affluence or poverty, color, sex, ethnicity and the like. And in accord with this noble blindness, His Honor will conduct himself in the court of law. It is as though the saying were incised on a heart that ever so slowly (or not so slowly) turns to stone.

This or that judge – let us grant him this (a large grant perhaps): he was once a good man, probably of middling talent and character. Grant him this, too: before he donned the robes, he would not willfully destroy or injure another. Indeed, his life could have turned in a far different direction; he could have risen to a mild eminence, become a small landowner, a workman unashamed. He might have kept a children's school or a neighborhood store, dependable and cheerful and kind of heart.

None of these. Honor came his way; he was named judge. He thought not to become a hangman, a harrier, a harpy. But shortly after the swearing-in, a blindfold descended on his eyes. The law blinded the keeper of the law. In honoring the law of the land, he ignored or forgot or came to despise justice. And in time the law brought him low. He became all the above: hangman, harrier, harpy.

So the king is brought low, lower than his victim Daniel. He had given no thought to the awful implication of his edict – that it might well bring his trusted friend to ruin. Now, after the fact, how is he to save Daniel? And if that is not possible, how can he, in spite of his affection, punish Daniel – and capitally at that?

Cynical, his henchmen goad him with his plight. "Know, O king, it is a law…no interdict or ordinance which the king establishes can be changed."

"I must uphold my oath of office." The king's charge echoes on the tongues of judges, time and again. It is a plea (truth told, a kind of guilty plea). We have seen it first hand. And the recalling is not sweet; it is of a Hitlerian judge doing his job. The law slowly (or not so slowly) throttles the keeper of the law.

Judge. There is no public office quite like this one. Other officials in other offices are required to play god in a pantheon of gods, each jostling for place, edgy and proud. But a judge is a god. He need never jostle his peers, or be jostled.

For each needs the other. And as a body, all are eminently useful, indeed indispensable to the prospering of the entire pantheon of empire. Each judge renders the judgment of the others justified. The play on words is delicious. This is a requirement of office. There is no imperial crime, no war, no larceny, no cover-up so outrageous that a judge cannot cleanse it of filth, make it presentable, shrug its malice away, deflect its consequence.

And the obverse is also true: no crime is so small as to evade the sternest, gimlet-eyed scrutiny. Indeed, small-bore crime is the specialty, ferociously pursued, of the urban courts of America. Welfare cheats! drug users! neighborhood nuisances! boom-box players! spitters in subways! pissers in public! – let these tremble in their boots.

A further requirement of office. A judge must be willing, ready and able, to criminalize those who declare the law of the land to be in conflict with justice, and who act in accord with their conviction. Conscience, Bible, international law? Out, damned spot!

Natural selection, I reflect, comes strongly to the rescue of judges; or perhaps it is environment. Whatever the resource, it is clear if a judge is to shine, he must be adaptable as a blowfish or a chameleon. In public, before the media, in court ("my court," by no means "yours," or worse, "ours") the required demeanor is stern and upright. In chambers, depending on occasion and, of course, off the record, he may roll an eye and trim a sail to the following or leading winds, to the political weather or the prospering of sponsors.

Thus a question arises: to whom is this or that judge indebted? The question is impertinent, so it must be posed. He is in debt to his sponsors, to their system of violence and rapacity and war, to their concave-convex scheme of wealth and misery. Which is to say, he is in debt to a system of law and order. He owes no debt to the law or justice of God. Or so he concludes, and so judges.

The gods he venerates fill his sails with wind, ensuring (for them and himself) a prosperous voyage. Those winds also have a voice; they are demons of suggestion. They whisper, "There are stowaways aboard, potential scuttlers of the ship of state." These must be discovered and put in chains.

The judge's patrons, it goes without saying, keep close watch over juridical behaviors. Those to whom debts come due include good tax-paying citizens; then, depending on the level of judgeship, corporate masters (those principalities of first rank); then bankers, international cartels, political hacks local or national (including the supreme patron, the president), speculators, wheelers and dealers in arms and in other properties immense or modest. Dealers finally, as the Book of Revelation grimly has it, in "human souls" (Rev. 18:13).

Such hardly disinterested parties tend somewhat to an irritated demanding. They have a thousand eyes; they keep careful account of the behavior of His Honor. Accountability! And questions, questions. Does His Truculence order removed from the public scene (indeed, when required, from this world) in strict accord with the law, those duly convicted? Does he protect and vindicate the inviolate character of property – a godling valued above every earthly reality? Does he exercise a fitting severity against those who challenge the secrecy and hegemony of installations of war; above all, of those places where nuclear war is in preparation? Does he deliver, as the occasion demands, stentorian denunciations of criminals, welfare cheats, drug users, not to speak of vagrants, disturbers, trespassers, pissers, the wantonly homeless who devalue by their very presence fair public places? Is he the advocate of long and longer prison terms? Does he take into account the superior sensibilities, even amid infrequent "lapses," of the wealthy? And does he likewise respond with required sternness to the effronteries and crudities of the poor?

Let us put matters in another way, forensically. At the behest of the principalities, a judge must be willing to declare black white, and white black; must render the ungodly godly – and vice versa. This is in fact the law he is sworn to honor – the law of the land.

In the confrontation of Daniel and Belshazzar, the point at issue was "the law of the Medes and Persians." In later centuries, among other niceties of "law of the land," one recalls the blood-purity laws of Hitler. And in our time and place, the "no trespass" laws protecting governmental and military crimes.

Law of the land, law of the land! Incant it, incense it, lave it in asperges,* fall prostrate before it. The only law, the supreme law, the law outlawing all other law. Speak not of conscience, summon not your biblical word, presume not to invoke the law of the nations, speak no more of urgent necessity, of tradition, of divine or human fonts of light. You would quote the Bible in your defense? Out of order! Irrelevant!

This is the law, which I, a judge, am sworn to promulgate and enforce. You, the accused, stand in the dock. I define you, in accord with the law. You are a being of two dimensions only, a citizen of this time and this nation. The two "frame" you (wryly, in more senses than one?). According to the law you are a citizen, and no more.

But do you, judge, dare add – I am a citizen of a sour political climate, the witness of atrocious wars, a friend of the homeless – protesting before your bar the ongoing judicial

*Asperges – the ceremony of sprinkling with holy water.

cover-up of high crime? Irrelevant! Whether you, the defendant, are religiously inclined – a priest, a professional, or a parent, whether you are endowed with conscience or prescient as to the Bible – it is all irrelevant.

The defendant is a Christian? Conscious of faith as a preeminent calling, a tradition precious beyond life itself? Would dare invoke, if allowed, the One who judges judges? The gavel falls. Irrelevant! Not here, not now. Not in my court!

The law of the land. And the outcome? The accused is either destroyed, or declared immaculate. Janus-faced, it plays hangman and savior both. Daniel and his kind stand before a very metaphysician, before a god. He pounds his gavel, and reality is shaken to the core.

In a Virginia Courtroom

Like a grey-faced
god almighty, fallen
in decrepitude,
Judge Grimesly
doles out days in purgatory.
Pity him.
These fresh-faced virtuous lawbreakers
tear him apart.
Fearless, merciless
they plant a bomb
in his vitals, like a bomb
in a briefcase,
then snapped shut.
Or one of these days
like a shot black bird
he will fly apart.

D. B.

The egg of reality cracks. Someone dies; a new creation springs. It is you, reborn – or you, reduced to ash. But whatever transpires, whatever heavy payment is exacted, whatever bright exoneration shines, your former life vanishes and your being is reborn.

The law. The word is like an impermeable enclosure, a death camp, like the prison it thrusts one into. What a heavy claim it wields; how it throttles! According to the claim, it encompasses the length, breadth, and depth of conscience itself. It comes to this: the human cannot be otherwise understood than "under the law." The yoke of the law presses hard, crushes. To this point, the claim of the law is one with the claim of death itself, as Paul realized (Rom. 7:7–12). But back to our story:

Daniel 6:14–16 The emotions of the actors are now curiously reversed. The king, we are told, is heavily distressed. But Daniel suffers no such burden.

We have here a kind of diagnostic irony, much to the point of events of our own day. As a judge, the king is endowed with life and death power. But Daniel, no ordinary accused, stands before him. The verdict of guilt has brought an unlikely outcome: peace to the victim, yet to the king no peace at all – only emotional turbulence.

For this irony to stand revealed, each – judge and defendant – need only play his part; "do," as is said, "his job." Let the judge, weak in principle and captive to the law, lord it over. And the accused? He or she need only be conscious, beyond need of proof or contention, of the virtue of the cause at issue. Then all good things will follow; a radiant demeanor, a peaceable soul, a legacy of unviolated hope.

Daniel 6:16 Daniel is condemned and led away, the prey of the royal lions. And a curious prayer follows him, uttered by his executioner: "May your God, whom you serve continually, deliver you" – a strange unaccustomed piety, seemingly tainted by cowardice and self interest. The king would fain preserve the life of Daniel, but he would also be king. Which is to say (though never by such as he) he is enslaved to the law. The king has made himself a god, and the god has failed. So the king invokes the God of Daniel. We have seen it since. The king is cornered into condemning an honorable man; now God must be invoked, to supply magically for the default. Behold the ploy. Failing to do justice, one hands over the work of justice to whatever deity.

Empty pietism, bad faith, lame prayer, and the incantation – in avoidance of plain moral duty – of a god who is misconceived of as a kind of bottled genie in service to fools and their follies. A debilitated coward holds office. Therefore a god must be uncorked and play instant surrogate.

Daniel 6:17–19 Shortly, the royal prayer is revealed for what it is – a washing of hands. Poor divided man! The king commences vigorously to oversee the execution he was unwilling to avert. Fevers and chills! He seals Daniel's fate, then retires to the palace, a Macbeth disintegrating before our eyes. The night wears on. The king was "fasting…and sleep fled from him."

Daniel 6:20–23 The rest is history, enshrined in stone and paint, in text and dance and music – the imagination of the tribe is never done with it. How the king arose at dawn, sleepless, morose (as one imagines), and in a panic of moral disarray hastened to the leonine lair. How he there found our hero unscathed, standing amid the great beasts, and they sublimely subdued. How Daniel, in command of the moment of truth, no reproof or anger on his tongue, reassured the discomfited monarch. The simple attribution of his well being is made to God's angel, who "stopped the mouth of the lions, and they have done me no ill."

A delightful ancient midrash has the king turning, on the moment, against Daniel's detractors. According to this version, they accuse Daniel of surreptitiously feeding the lions prior to his being condemned; thus offering by preemption a saving substitute in place of his own too solid flesh.

Daniel 6:25–28 We have a rousing Constantinian ending. By order of the converted king, subjects to the ends of the earth must immediately, religiously come to heel before the One who has delivered the prophet. "Let all people tremble and fear before the God of Daniel." Well, perhaps.

Daniel Also Dreams; The Four Beasts

The Book of Daniel

7 In the first year of King Belshazzar of Babylon, Daniel had a
dream and visions of his head as he lay in bed. Then he wrote
down the dream: 2 I, Daniel, saw in my vision by night the four
winds of heaven stirring up the great sea, 3 and four great beasts
came up out of the sea, different from one another. 4 The first was
like a lion and had eagles' wings. Then, as I watched, its wings were
plucked off, and it was lifted up from the ground and made to
stand on two feet like a human being; and a human mind was
given to it. 5 Another beast appeared, a second one, that looked like
a bear. It was raised up on one side, had three tusks in its mouth
among its teeth and was told, "Arise, devour many bodies!" 6 After
this, as I watched, another appeared, like a leopard. The beast had
four wings of a bird on its back and four heads; and dominion was
given to it. 7 After this I saw in the visions by night a fourth beast,
terrifying and dreadful and exceedingly strong. It had great iron
teeth and was devouring, breaking in pieces, and stamping what
was left with its feet. It was different from all the beasts that preceded it, and it had ten horns. 8 I was considering the horns, when
another horn appeared, a little one coming up among them; to
make room for it, three of the earlier horns were plucked up by the
roots. There were eyes like human eyes in this horn, and a mouth
speaking arrogantly.

9 As I watched, thrones were set in place,
    and an Ancient One took his throne,
his clothing was white as snow,
    and the hair of his head like pure wool;
his throne was fiery flames,
    and its wheels were burning fire.
10 A stream of fire issued
    and flowed out from his presence.
A thousand thousands served him,
    and ten thousand times ten thousand
    stood attending him.

The court sat in judgment,
and the books were opened.

[11]I watched then because of the noise of the arrogant words that the
horn was speaking. And as I watched, the beast was put to death,
and its body destroyed and given over to be burned with fire. [12]As
for the rest of the beasts, their dominion was taken away, but their
lives were prolonged for a season and a time. [13]As I watched in the
night visions,

I saw one like a human being
coming with the clouds of heaven.
And he came to the Ancient One
and was presented before him.
[14]To him was given dominion
and glory and kingship,
that all peoples, nations, and languages
should serve him.
His dominion is an everlasting dominion
that shall not pass away,
and his kingship is one that shall never be destroyed.

[15]As for me, Daniel, my spirit was troubled within me, and the visions of my head terrified me. [16]I approached one of the attendants
to ask him the truth concerning all this. So he said that he would
disclose to me the interpretation of the matter: [17]"As for these four
great beasts, four kings shall arise out of the earth. [18]But the holy
ones of the Most High shall receive the kingdom and possess the
kingdom forever – forever and ever."

[19]Then I desired to know the truth concerning the fourth beast,
which was different from all the rest, exceedingly terrifying, with its
teeth of iron and claws of bronze, and which devoured and broke
in pieces, and stamped what was left with its feet; [20]and concerning
the ten horns that were on its head, and concerning the other horn,
which came up and to make room for which three of them fell
out – the horn that had eyes and a mouth that spoke arrogantly,
and that seemed greater than the others. [21]As I looked, this horn

made war with the holy ones and was prevailing over them, 22 until
the Ancient One came; then judgment was given for the holy ones
of the Most High, and the time arrived when the holy ones gained
possession of the kingdom.

23 This is what he said: "As for the fourth beast,

there shall be a fourth kingdom on earth
    that shall be different from all the other kingdoms;
it shall devour the whole earth,
    and trample it down, and break it to pieces.
24 As for the ten horns,
out of this kingdom ten kings shall arise,
    and another shall arise after them.
This one shall be different from the former ones,
    and shall put down three kings.
25 He shall speak words against the Most High,
    shall wear out the holy ones of the Most High,
    and shall attempt to change the sacred seasons and the law;
and they shall be given into his power
    for a time, two times, and half a time.
26 Then the court shall sit in judgment,
    and his dominion shall be taken away,
    to be consumed and totally destroyed.
27 The kingship and dominion
    and the greatness of the kingdoms under the whole heaven
    shall be given to the people of
    the holy ones of the Most High;
their kingdom shall be an everlasting kingdom,
    and all dominions shall serve and obey them."

28 Here the account ends. As for me, Daniel, my thoughts greatly terrified me, and my face turned pale; but I kept the matter in my mind.

Daniel Also Dreams; The Four Beasts

Daniel 7:1 ff. If the previous episodes are grist for myth makers, this one offers an abundance of meat for academic molars. Meat for the strong above all; the identity of the mysterious figure "one like the son of man" (literally "the human one") in verse 13. Do we have here a messianic figure? The deliverer of his people? A quasi-divine one? The prophet himself? A forerunner of Jesus? A personification of all saints? All or any of these?

Speluncation, speculation. With these, if not careful, we drown the seeing eye. Let us recall: the eye of faith looks to scripture not for the furrowing of the academic brow, but for the food that gives life. It can hardly be out of order then, to underscore again the message of the book of Daniel. As suggested heretofore, two themes are stressed. One: the kingdoms of earth (the superpowers of that time and our own), persecutors and killers of the faithful – these are unmasked; more, they are declared redundant to God's grand design. They will have an end. The end is judgment. Time is granted the empires; the sense is of a more or less reluctant, temporary allowance, a doling out of a lifeline of time – this together with a stern watchfulness, their works of terror lying under the scrutiny of God. And two: in that crepuscular "meantime," the time of terror and of the tormentor, the saints are summoned to stand firm in faith and endurance.

An irony is implied in the opening of the dream sequence granted to Daniel; it is striking, delightful. Formerly Daniel acted as interpreter, bringing the high and mighty to earth with a thump. Now he is drawn into the dream life of the kings. He himself will have need of the service he rendered others with such consummate skill. Someone to tell the meaning of mysterious, afflicting images. But who shall help the truth teller reach a deeper truth? No one of earth; certainly not the failed necromancers of the king. Not even the companions of the early episodes, edifying as they are, at one with Daniel in prayer – or danger. None of these. An angel, no less. We have a puzzle, a koan, a tease worthy of Isak Dinesen or Gabriel Garcia Marquez. Behold, an angel strangely inhabits the dream of Daniel and unlocks it from within.

His first dream paints a vast canvas of successive kingdoms. Each appears under a symbol, a beast. An "as if" animal, a dream bestiary that includes details: it is as though human characteristics were grafted on animal anatomy. The images are a kind of patchwork of imagination. A series of never-never beasts stalk the earth, beasts never once existing on land or sea. A lion with wings of eagles, a bear with three bloodied ribs in his teeth, a winged leopard. And finally, a fourth appears. Its guise is hallucinatory, grisly. It renders the seer speechless with horror.

We are in the presence of Truth. And the truth is all but unendurable. To be sure, the imperial beings present themselves as normal; more, as virtuous, benign. (Such self delusion is, of course, greatly to their interest.) But Daniel's dream offers a truth beyond the reach of propaganda and self aggrandizement. Only, it would seem, through a nightmarish fusing of incompatible, even impossible oppositions can the uniquely bestial quality of the superpowers be conveyed. To Daniel is proffered the truth; and through him, to ourselves.

Gorgeously, menacingly, the kingdoms parade before the prophet, who stands there appalled. They show their true visage. To the inner eye of the dreamer, it is plain bestial.

It is worth noting, and instructive as well, that as historic realities, the Big Four are of merely taxidermic interest today. What is striking is the unrelenting scriptural judgment that rests on these sovereignties. In each we behold, par excellence, the social and political "dwellers upon the earth." Which is to say, according to Daniel, these four are obsessed with the conquest of time and this world. As such they inevitably clash with God and God's people. In the words of a later oracle, they "make war on the saints" (Rev. 13). As each appears, rises, and finally vanishes from the earth, their resemblance to another is striking. In sanguinary appetite, envy, guile, wanton violence, ghoulish ideology, each is like a mirror held to a mirror in a house of horrors. They are dissimilar only in degree of criminality.

Is Daniel the exiled Jew in need of instruction in these matters? Perhaps in less need than ourselves, whose faith is singularly bereft of moral clarity – so often diminished to conformity, to a shrug before "things as they are." Against such the empire hardly need unsheathe a sword. It offers instead a stupefying diet of bread and circuses. So, consuming and content, multitudes live safe and die sorry.

Perhaps from another angle also, Daniel is a figure of moment for ourselves, requiring as we do the brusque nudge of a dream, a clap to the shoulder. His princely status, exile or no, Jew or no, his exalted place in court – this, as he knows well, is a dangerous circumstance, easily accelerated to a soft spin and a drowning complicity.

The beasts arise from the sea, that chaotic and unappeasable element. They arise, then they vanish; one empire succeeds another, "one differs from another." Yet all are alike, superhuman and subhuman at once, in conduct intensely, virulently at odds with God and God's justice.

The first of the realms, the Babylonian, is endowed with eagle's wings. It soars above the human condition, in its own estimate an altogether unique being, unaccountable before the law, superior to ordinary mortals. It is moreover, leonine, and "lifted up from the ground and made to stand on its feet like a man." Daniel knows "the mind of a man was given to it." Carnivorous, that is, and rational at once. According to the imperial logic, killing makes perfect sense; indeed, it is endemic to the appetite for power. To its way of thinking (this empire is a great one for taking thought), military conquest, a society of slaves and masters, economic piracy – these clear a path in the worldly thicket of contention. A lion as symbol, a pride of lions; the king of the beasts indeed.

The second, the Median, resembles a bear, voracious and on the prowl. Indeed, a prey is lodged between its teeth, slain and half devoured. And an instruction is given it (as though it were in need of such! as though such a monster were not already in process of masticating its victim, of enacting the command): "Arise, devour much flesh." The word is peremptory and has no indicated source. Who, what may be thought to issue such an instruction?

No one, no witness, no fellow carnivore is named. None is required. The words arise from within, from its voracious genesis, its own guts. The imperative hangs on the air, self contained, self justifying. It points to the necessary evil, the lesser evil. Thus the instruction approves every declaration of war, every incursion, every slaughter, whether in progress or in plan.

The angel of Revelation joins the war-banquet in a summons to the "birds of the air" (Rev. 19:17–19), to "Come! gather together for the great feast God has prepared for you. You are to eat the flesh of kings, of commanders and warriors, of horses and their riders, the flesh of all men, the free and the slave, the small and the great." It is the scavenger birds who are invited to banquet on the stinking flesh of humans, after the battle. The birds are a surrogate image of those who fatten off the profits of war; they are flesh eating, they seek after human offal. Thus war, thus those who wage it, profit from it; and thus its inglorious close.

And immediately, from banquet to battle: "Then I saw the beast and the kings of the earth, and the armies they had mustered to do battle with the One riding the horse, and with his army." The kings are in concert with one named "the beast." The malevolent presence of the latter is a stunning biblical insight. War, that is, surpasses all human machination and prospect of advantage. Someone, Something, ever so silently joins the imperial war makers. Whether invited or not, no matter. The beast is present, provoking, nudging, suggesting a "just cause."

Thus the kings (and today NATO or SEATO or whatever mutual pact) are linked with an ally at once invisible and invincible: the beast. The spirit of death rides with them; one must almost say, rides them, and hard. Another than they holds firm the reins of history, or so purposes.

Another capital point. The "enemy" of this monstrous collusion is Christ, the One who also rides the terrain of earth. Whose believing community, moreover, is in perennial conflict against the spirit of death and its human servitors, the death-dealers.

Talk about total war and its outcome! With vivacious, lethal irony, the angel deflates the glories of battle. War is, all said, a feast of cannibals, an obscenity at once subhuman and dehumanizing.

The image summons to mind the imperative of the imperium, the conscienceless urge of the blood, the self assurance, the instinct, the deadly tradition, the itch, the quick solution, the enticement of memory and ancestry, the whisper of dark minds. The skill, the kill, the sword that carves a swath, begetting and maintaining world empery.

The third kingdom is Persian. A brisk summary is offered: a leopard, four wings, four heads. The number denotes a totality, a system, a self sufficiency. In its own estimate, its closed universe of pride and possession, its guarded borders, this realm considers itself ultimate, immortal, impregnable. It appears upon earth, rules and lords it over lesser realms, makes a fanfare upon the hour. "And dominion was given it." The fantastic has become a kind of horrid cliché; the third kingdom tiresomely resembles the preceding two. It is passive, be it noted, for all its ravening and raging. Dominion and control are simply handed over like a cloak of iron – or a curse – from one to the next.

Contrary to bombast and trumpeted rhetoric, this realm too passes. To the laughter of God and the derision of the martyrs.

The fourth beast – what are we to make of it; what does Daniel and his dream make of it? What did he see? It stops the heart. It is as though an interior censor warned the prophet (warned ourselves): this is too much. Here, draw a blank. Something unspeakable, something that resembles nothing known to creation. We are told that here his dream symbols fail him and fall away.The beast is simply itself – a beast, a generic horror, predatory, exceeding all, forebears, descendants, peers, in quality and scope of malevolence.

In a sense, the imaginative stutter of Daniel gives place for the truth. The fourth beast is literally unimaginable for this reason; he unites in himself the contradictory, metaphysically incompatible patchwork – the dream work (better, the nightmare work) of the preceding three. As kingdom succeeds kingdom, the new genesis not only surpasses the old in wickedness. It consumes and grows upon the raw meat of the past. It seizes upon prior technique and conduct, whether of war, exploitation, enslavement.

The fourth kingdom arises. It is as though the world were reduced to an abandoned, smoking battlefield, strewn with the dead. The unspeakable newborn proceeds to dismember, analyze, consume the corpses of its predecessors. Their substance, brain and brawn (and their technological savvy!) vitalize, become horridly incarnate in the last and worst of their kind.

The last empire, Alexander's, is nonetheless of a different order than the prior three. Ten horns, ten incumbents to the throne, we are told, succeed one another in a single line. Then an eleventh emerges, smaller, eyed, voluble. For the first time in the dream of Daniel, the figure of an empire yields before a single human. This one will embody, in the scope and depth and breadth of his malfeasance, the social pathology of all empires. This one "spoke grandiloquently," blaspheming and arrogant.

A certain Antiochus is named (a figure who but for his fervent criminality is undistinguished in the imperial line). This one is known solely, purely for evil. Antiochus IV – the quintessential enemy of the saints, the enemy contemporary to Daniel. He is the subject of the plenary judgment of God (Dan. 7:25). This tyrant, intent on wiping out the faith and culture of his victims, abolishes the Sabbath and the sacred feasts: "He will utter words against the Most High and make light of sacred times, and the law and the saints will be delivered into his hands for a time, twice time and half a time."

Daniel 7:9–14 To revert, Daniel stands as yet within the dream, which now takes a new tack, an imagery of the end time. The kingdoms, their apparatus, their crimes, have issued (like the primordial "beast" of Revelation) from the waters of chaos. They have occupied time and place, and vanished. There remains only judgment.

A Mirror for the Twentieth Century

A coffin bearing the face of a boy
A book
Written on the belly of a crow
A wild beast hidden in a flower
A rock
Breathing with the lungs of a lunatic;
This is it;
This is the Twentieth Century.
Ali Ahmad Sa'id

So we are told of thrones, and an ancient one seated. (The description of the deity here is wondrously transposed, in Revelation 1, to the risen Jesus.) The book lies open; the scene unfolds; the weighing, wanting, and sentencing of the nations. To quote G. B. Caird, from his *Eschatology and Politics:*

> ...[The scene] is set in the midst of world history. The case before the court is an appeal from the plaintiff Israel...for redress against the tyrannical treatment she has received at the hands of successive world empires...The divine court of appeal, we are to understand, keeps close watch over the corruptions of imperial power, and in due course removes it from those who abuse it with bestial cruelty – in order to bestow it on those capable of wielding it with humanity.

Judgment – a constant theme in the Jewish testament. And not only "the nations" are subject to the scrutiny of God (Ps. 9:7–8). Be it noted (especially in light of dire events today) that Israel too, a victim transformed, is all but absorbed in the leaven of "the nations," and as such will herself be judged (Amos 2:6 ff.).

The fourth beast is convicted, dispossessed, and destroyed. Its crimes have become literally intolerable; evil had all but emptied the veins of creation. Now the seer may breathe deep once more, in exhaustion and relief. This fourth was, in every sense, the final kingdom of earth. Time and its tyrants will have ending. The final empire was to be (will be) replaced by the realm of God.

As for the preceding three, they are granted a reprieve of sorts. Their domination was taken from them. Their falling short has become, strangely, their only hope. A reprieve is granted; they come to represent (Dan. 7:27) the nations that one day, through the saints, will do homage to God.

Now opens the splendid vision of the "One coming with the clouds of heaven, likened to the human One." The origin of this mysterious being is in stark contrast to that of the four beasts. They emerge from primary chaos, to create chaos in the world. He on the other hand is a heavenly figure, transcendent, holy. He bears a divine vocation and so receives of God reward and honor.

Much contention, like the swirling thunders that encompass Daniel, has shaken the visionary throne. Who is this one? He is identified variously, richly. And, one thinks, all to the good, an image of the many and the one. He calls to mind the "suffering servant" of Isaiah, or perhaps the personification of the holy people (in Dan. 7:27 like promises are made to him and them). He is taken also for the Messiah; the "human one," icon and leader of the holy people. Or he is a symbol of the Jewish Maccabees, thus Saint Ephram. (A strange attribution, one thinks, since the Maccabean line, except for the martyrs in their midst, was hardly more admirable than the kings here under judgment!) And finally, the Human One stands pristine and promised, a surrogate for the Holy One of the Christian testament. Jesus assumes the title to himself (Mark 14:62); his interlocutors are given to understand that he is someone who mysteriously surpasses the human condition.*

Daniel 7:15–18 Daniel remains lost in dream, through verse 28. And a dream within a dream! We note that the interpretation of the angel is, delightfully enough, imbedded in the dream itself. This is the dream-laden meaning of the dream; the hope of Daniel and his kind is blessed. The promise is intact; one day the saints will take possession of an eternal realm.

The four rulers, on the other hand, are creatures of time; transient, doomed to undergo the death they inflict on others. It may be that these comprise in their social body all evils possible to the principalities and their human cronies. With a heavy heart we grant them that, knowing that their fury and fanfare come at length to nothing.

Hearken then to their history, and especially to its outcome, Daniel is urged. No matter the pretensions, small matter the cruelties and idolatries. The tyrants are no more than arrogant outsiders, pretenders to the throne of God, figures of delay, hypothetical, redundant, loitering beyond their allotted time. Blind and unwitting, they are like iron figures in a clockworks gone awry. They tell the time wrong. The Bible places them aright. They linger about the fringes of history, pretending mightily to make history. But scripture quietly weaves the pattern of true history, the story of the saints and martyrs. On the

*Cf. corresponding notes in *Le Bible de Jérusalem.*

others and their works and pomps, the book of Daniel casts a cold eye. In no sense protagonists, they are nudged to one side, to the wings of the drama. Their victims, ah! these are the true protagonists, the heroes.

These great ones are slaves, drawing water up from the well of time. Or they are likened to the base clay of Genesis, out of which God fashions the future. So God is patient with them and their crimes. But not forever. To their peers, as to their victimized and thoughtless votaries, they bulk hugely, jostling for pride of place. In truth, theirs is a mere "meantime," a gap. In that interim God conceals, then ever so gradually and patiently (the saints too must be patient), reveals the divine purpose.

No need to add that the royal consciousness disagrees hugely with the biblical deflation. Kings hold another version of their role in history. More, they have at disposal sycophant historians, artists, singers, sculptors, poets, builders of monuments and arches, all commandeered to spread abroad the imperial version of achievement and renown. In sum, the task of these is to deliver to the centuries the imperial myth – the royal ego, intact, conflated, larger than life.

The community of faith stands outside the myth, skeptical, questioning. Again and again, scripture and its heroes witness to another outcome. Daniel stands there, at prayer or in contention, witnessing to that purpose, the will of Jahweh for humankind.

The tyrants are of interest to the prophets only because their rise, momentary flourishing, and fall illustrate the truth of God's urgent word to the saints: Believe, trust, endure; God is faithful.

Daniel 7:19–28 Daniel is of course most concerned with the tyrant of his own lifetime, Antiochus IV. This one mounted the worst assault in history against Jewish survival (see 1 Macc. 1:20–63). A tyrant who passes belief, he moved and removed high priests, looted the temple treasury, ordered savage reprisals against the helpless population of Jerusalem, and erected as a sign of his authority the dreaded Akra (a citadel for foreign troops, a refuge for apostates, and a conspicuous symbol of oppression) within the shadow of the temple. In addition to all this, as opposition to his policies gained in strength, he proscribed the torah and the sacrifices, outlawed the traditional customs, and persecuted to death those who defied these measures. In this program of enforced Hellenization, everything that bore the mark of traditional Judaism was uprooted. But the crowning act of blasphemy, the challenge to God, occurred in 167 BCE, when Antiochus set up the "abomination of desolation" in the temple and ordered the offering of sacrifices to Zeus (Dan. 11:31). It was not until three years later that the blasphemy was removed, the temple cleansed, and the lights lit.*

Finally (Dan. 7:28) we note Daniel's trouble of spirit on behalf of his troubled people. His heart is heavy. Has he seen too much, too quickly? In any case he seems disinclined, at least in the short run, to speak of the dire matters that have unfolded before him.

While Daniel pauses (to take stock of his situation?) we might also pause to recall themes which the book underscores. The revelation offers an apocalyptic critique of the times and the rulers of earth. Its tone is harsh, unyielding, biting, a political message of the highest order. Its message is of import first of all to the persecuted: the promise endures, though the skies be shaken.

*Robert A. Anderson, *Signs and Wonders.*

Of moment as well (even if not often considered) is the gift which the oracles of Daniel offer the rulers themselves. Shall they too be saved, who have sinned so bloodily? And if salvation is offered them as well, whence will it come, if not through courageous truth tellers, those who utter God's word even in the threat and onset of death?

Then – as to prayer: prior to facing the king's fury the community falls to a sustaining prayer. They intercede on behalf of the king: May he come to a better mind, not only for our sake but for his own! Talk about the political responsibility of believers.

Much scholarship has gone awry here, implying or stating that Daniel's apocalyptic sense led him – and will lead us as well – to withdrawal from the world. To the contrary (as though it required saying), "Daniel's interest in and allegiance to the heavenly world serves to sharpen his confrontation with the kingdoms of the earth" (Collins, *Daniel*). Confronting the powers, the faithful are to remain patient and nonviolent; by the sword of the spirit they will withstand. Daniel's prayer and public conduct are clear on the matter.

In our book, as in Revelation, there occur battle scenes galore, earthly and heavenly. The imagery is usual in apocalyptic writings. The conflicts are often as not cast in celestial images. This, as we have suggested, lays a judgment "from above" (which is to say, from the eminence of a higher law that that "of the land") against the tyrants.

It is worth recalling that, biblically understood, war on earth is waged against Jahweh. It is as though this or that tyrant took up arms to storm high heaven, declaring hostility against a divine order that commends peace and compassion on earth. God is the enemy.

The Book of Daniel shifts frequently to far different

scenes than those of imperial carnage. It must be; relief must be offered, if the saints are to persevere. God's order is honored, verified by the faithful, in rejection of the dominion of the beasts (Dan. 7). Politics again, and responsibility toward the living, are altruistically shown by the persecuted community itself.

So we have the biblical view of history, and the regal view. And between the two it would seem that no peaceable coexistence is possible. The godlings and their gods, an insuperable show. Leading the triumphant procession of the four realms is the *vexilla regis,* the emperor's banner; then come chariots and war horses. Captives and slaves bring up the rear. Such honor, such glory! Citizens are dazzled, who has seen the like?

A triumphant arch is erected at the gate of the imperial city; coins are struck; a proclamation is trumpeted, announcing the divinity of the ruler.

History is thus defined, dramatized, canonized. It is the "ascent of man." The ideal political form is the empire; the ideal human the male warrior; the ideal task "service" of the emperor. And the service at the peak denotes military induction – which is to say, conquest and killing. And if for sake of the royal progress the road now and again proves rough and uphill, if at times mountains must be leveled and valleys filled, if many must die and much misery ensue, why then, let it occur!

A news break, the item from *The New York Times*:

> Thousands have thyroid cancer from atomic tests…Fallout from nuclear blasts at the Nevada test site near Las Vegas may have caused 10,000 to 75,000 thyroid cancers, 70 percent of which have not yet been diagnosed, the National Cancer Institute said today. Three-quarters of those cases are expected to develop in people who were younger than 5 at the time of

> exposure, which occurred mainly in 1952–1957...Medical experts say that about 10 percent of such cancers are fatal. There were few, if any, Americans in the contiguous 48 states at the time that were not exposed to some level of fallout...
>
> *August 2, 1997*

Must the innocent fall ill and die? All is accounted for, compensated for by the ever accumulating power of empire, by the booty of conquered lands and world markets – as well as by the honors that accrue, whether to the nuclear scientists, the warriors, or their king. Indeed, honor conferred on the leaders spells honor to all. And the huge labors required for raising monuments, public buildings, shrines, cenotaphs? There are slaves and captives and exiles for that.

Then the biblical view, the view of Daniel and his companions. History is crisis; it is a Passion. From the perspective of the poor this is the truest view, the way it seems always to be. Apocalypticism collapses the meaning of history into a stark choice given each succeeding generation: choose between the hope of life and side with the suffering, and the legacy of death administrated by the stewards of good order (Matt. 23:29–31). The cosmic battle between "histories" forces one to choose, politically and socially. There is no neutrality. Faith must choose what history it stands in solidarity with, and crisis is the soil in which that faith grows.*

And at the epicenter of choice stands Daniel, the classical outsider-insider. Unease and tension lie heavy on him as he prepares to carry his case – the plight of his people – before the tyrant. He is hardly starry eyed: he knows what is pos-

*Ched Myers, "Apocalyptic," unpublished essay.

sible and what not. Granted, they are enslaved; all the same he will have justice, a modicum of justice – or at the least a mitigation of outrageous injustice. A modicum. This, or he is prepared to die.

That the efforts may well exact his life is hardly an illusion. Kings, rulers of every stripe, presidents, shahs, generals, these are a prickly species, as we have seen again and again – and by no means in the book of Daniel only. (Nor in the Bible only!) The insider on one day can on another be summarily thrust into outer darkness. What these martinets, tossed hither and yon by the shifting weathers of event – what they will brook, even from a trusted confidant – on what occasion a regal mood will darken, no one can well predict. There are furnaces fired for such as Daniel, and dens of great lions.

He counsels his soul, and his companions, to a revolutionary patience (a phrase borrowed in our day from the Vietnamese, who know something of such matters). We have noted the sequence; prayer first, patient, perduring. Then on to action, in the breach, at risk of a deadly outcome. This is the sequence and formula of nonviolent resistance. For the parlous times of Daniel, for today.

The Time of Indignation, the Time of the End

The Book of Daniel

8 In the third year of the reign of King Belshazzar a vision appeared to me, Daniel, after the one that had appeared to me at
first. [2]In the vision I was looking and saw myself in Susa the capital,
in the province of Elam, and I was by the river Ulai. [3]I looked up
and saw a ram standing beside the river. It had two horns. Both
horns were long, but one was longer than the other, and the longer
one came up second. [4]I saw the ram charging westward and north-
ward and southward. All beasts were powerless to withstand it, and
no one could rescue from its power; it did as it pleased and became
strong.

[5]As I was watching, a male goat appeared from the west, coming
across the face of the whole earth without touching the ground.
The goat had a horn between its eyes. [6]It came toward the ram with
the two horns that I had seen standing beside the river, and it ran at
it with savage force. [7]I saw it approaching the ram. It was enraged
against it and struck the ram, breaking its two horns. The ram did
not have power to withstand it; it threw the ram down to the
ground and trampled upon it, and there was no one who could
rescue the ram from its power. [8]Then the male goat grew exceedingly great; but at the height of its power, the great horn was broken, and in its place there came up four prominent horns toward
the four winds of heaven.

[9]Out of one of them came another horn, a little one, which grew
exceedingly great toward the south, toward the east, and toward the
beautiful land. [10]It grew as high as the host of heaven. It threw
down to the earth some of the host and some of the stars, and
trampled on them. [11]Even against the prince of the host it acted
arrogantly; it took the regular burnt offering away from him and
overthrew the place of his sanctuary. [12]Because of wickedness, the
host was given over to it together with the regular burnt offering; it
cast truth to the ground, and kept prospering in what it did.
[13]Then I heard a holy one speaking, and another holy one said to

the one that spoke, "For how long is this vision concerning the
regular burnt offering, the transgression that makes desolate, and
the giving over of the sanctuary and host to be trampled?" [14]And he
answered him, "For two thousand three hundred evenings and
mornings; then the sanctuary shall be restored to its rightful state."

[15]When I, Daniel, had seen the vision, I tried to understand it.
Then someone appeared standing before me, having the appearance of a man, [16]and I heard a human voice by the Ulai, calling,
"Gabriel, help this man understand the vision." [17]So he came near
where I stood; and when he came, I became frightened and fell
prostrate. But he said to me, "Understand, O mortal, that the vision is for the time of the end."

[18]As he was speaking to me, I fell into a trance, face to the
ground; then he touched me and set me on my feet. [19]He said,
"Listen, and I will tell you what will take place later in the period of
wrath; for it refers to the appointed time of the end. [20]As for the
ram that you saw with the two horns, these are the kings of Media
and Persia. [21]The male goat is the king of Greece, and the great
horn between its eyes is the first king. [22]As for the horn that was
broken, in place of which four others arose, four kingdoms shall
arise from his nation, but not with his power.

[23]At the end of their rule,
    when the transgressions have reached their full measure,
a king of bold countenance shall arise,
    skilled in intrigue.
[24]He shall grow strong in power,
    shall cause fearful destruction,
    and shall succeed in what he does.
He shall destroy the powerful
    and the people of the holy ones.
[25]By his cunning he shall make deceit prosper under his hand,
    and in his own mind he shall be great.
Without warning he shall destroy many

and shall even rise up against the Prince of princes.
But he shall be broken,
and not by human hands.

26The vision of the evenings and the mornings that has been told is true. As for you, seal up the vision, for it refers to many days from now."

27So I, Daniel, was overcome and lay sick for some days; then I arose and went about the king's business. But I was dismayed by the vision and did not understand it.

The Time of Indignation, the Time of the End

Daniel 8:1–3 The chapter is rather exactly dated; some two years after the event just preceding. Date and placing are of import here, in view of the crucial nature of what is to be revealed.

The Persian ram Artaxerxes, we are told, has been challenged and defeated by the Macedonian goat, Alexander the Great. (We need not tarry over the symbols; they speak noisomely for themselves. Nor need wearisome details of war and rumor of war, alarums and excursions, detain us overlong. As has been noted, perhaps unto weariness, a central theme of our book is the rise and fall of tyrants. This latter by way of reminder and reassurance, then and now.)

In their reign these dubious eminences "magnify themselves exceedingly" (Dan. 8:8). It would seem that self delusion in far excess of the human measure is a congenital illness of imperial entities. A persistent mythology develops; themes of virtuous behavior and unassailable omnipotence proliferate. And for a time the myths prevail. Nothing or very little of truth prevails.

So today in the media, sound bites and headlines strongly imply that we ought to forget all "facts to the contrary." The uses of amnesia are sweet. Forget the slaughter of native peoples, incursions and invasions of the south continent and elsewhere. Forget the midnight assaults of Jim Crow, the detention of Nisei peoples in wartime. Forget medical experiments on prisoners. Forget the "down-winders," those citizens (including soldiers) who, exposed unknowingly to nuclear experimentation, grew mortally ill. Forget police rampaging against minority peoples and workers. Forget the quiet war of sanctions against Iraq (which have already cost the deaths of millions) and against Cuba. Forget the counter-intelligence crimes of the FBI brainchild, COINTELPRO. Forget the brazen unaccountability of the CIA.

In certain instances the law of the land is wonderfully adaptive. None of the above crimes is brought to the bar of justice. And at large, a mood of innocence is deepened by cultural mythology. The myth lauds to the skies the scions of a virtuous empire. It spins, too, a web of delusion. Thus: we North Americans have been generous and compassionate toward others, in a world which by and large remains ungrateful and unresponsive and, in many instances, unrepentantly hostile.

If the charade were a matter of mere posturing and play acting, we could leave the authorities to their blood sports. Alas, their excesses work catastrophic consequences abroad and at home.

Daniel 8:9 The two animal-kings are granted small attention in the oracle. Daniel turns away from their furious butting and rutting. Rather, the vision concentrates with horror on the "little horn," Antiochus IV, on his reprisals against Jerusalem and violation of the temple precincts. In such ways he devastates "the glorious land" and its people.

Daniel 8:10 The horn, "little" as it is (a kind of contemptuous gloss of Daniel?), "grows great." Nothing more dangerous than a bit actor determined on playing protagonist! This second-rate dynast pushes on, determined on a glorious rating in history. He rattles his arms and undertakes a war against heaven itself.

The vainglorious lout, we are told, "defied the Prince of Glory." We note a like theme in the Book of Revelation; there and here, apocalyptic insight lays bare a momentous conclusion. We have seen it before; imperial wars mount an assault on God by their very nature (Rev. 12:7–9). In the first instance they challenge the divine hegemony over creation. The wars are blasphemous. With a truly appalling vanity, their instigators play hobs with the divine self revelation – a God of love, compassion, and justice, announcing and commending peace on earth.

Endlessly, instinctively, with no definitive outcome, the goat and ram clash and rant and butt about. No winner, no end in sight. It is as though they were spasmodically possessed, as though they acted out, under instruction of demons, the drama of darkness and its prince, the demonic "other." As though they were fated to mime the un-god, the spirit of hatred, contempt, and injustice – the spirit of war on earth.

Back to verse 10: the wars, reaching to high heaven, cast down "some of the hosts of stars." The stars of heaven are symbols of people of faith, of martyrs, victimized by the tyrants throughout history (as in Matt. 13:43 and Rev. 12:4). These dwell in heaven, in anticipation and hope; thus they stand at the opposite zone of creation from the "dwellers upon the earth."

But wars are not waged merely against God's own. Worse, war is declared against the "Prince of the host" (Dan. 8:11). And this concretely, historically, with all deliberation. It comes to this appalling event. The temple is profaned, given over to idols. The "abomination of desolation" is installed there. (Daniel's account falls short; he cannot encompass the scope of the blasphemy or exhaust its horror. It is as though a stake had been driven in the heart of a people. As though its memory were permanently fixated upon the crime. So in more detail, 1 Macc. 1:54 ff. and 2 Macc. 6:1–11.)

Daniel 8:12 "And truth was cast to ground." A veiled reference, a kind of code language referring to a time of evil that lay beyond the power of words. These occurred: the truth of worship was trampled underfoot, as in 167 BCE, when an altar to Zeus was raised in the temple. The scandal was past bearing. And if worse could be imagined, it came to pass. A number of defections occurred within the believing community.

"The horn acted and prospered." Invariably both occur; a feverish energy suffuses the principalities. As for their human cronies, for a time they flourish beyond measure. And why not? The kings have the assurance of the "prince of this world" that the world and time are in his clutch, and that he is free to distribute his hegemony to those who "fall down and adore me" (Matt. 4:9). Therefore. The logic is from hell, and beyond refuting.

Daniel 8:13 Suddenly, against all expectation, the vision takes a charming, unique turn. Two angels appear. One to the other, these socratic spirits raise and answer the question that torments our seer Daniel: "How long..?" The question echoes age after age in scripture. It is like the cry, faint and unquenchable, of a parched ghost. A cry uttered time and again in Daniel, in the Psalms, in Job, in Revelation.

Here a specific evil is in question, the profanation of the sanctuary. But the query points also to a grander scene: to the definitive "end," the final intervention of God, the unraveling of our tangled history. The Event par excellence, that suffused the imagination of Christ with its charm, the time of banquet and harvest. And in the Hebrew prophets, a sterner note; the undoing of every human assumption and power, the unsealing of the book of judgment, the unmasking of dark majesties, the vindication of the martyrs, a blessing (at long last) traced upon the foreheads of the suffering faithful. Consolation after such desolation! These, and a rebuke and judgment spoken against every principality. And lest we forget (Luke 1:52–55), the irony upon irony of the Day: "the strong toppled from thrones, the lowly exalted, the rich sent away empty, the hungry filled with good things."

"How long?" The question issues most movingly of all from the tongues of the martyrs, strangely sequestered as they abide "under the altar" (Rev. 6:9). Though presumably dwelling in eternal life, the witnesses seek a meaning which continues to evade them, the meaning of such an end as their lives have endured. They would have sense made of their death, sense made of the injustice that destroyed them – and that continues, haunting, perennial, awful, to destroy their sisters and brothers.

These who cry out are witnesses to the Word of God; they died for the sake of its integrity. Now, under the altar of sacrifice, as though in some holding tank of this world (they have often been detained in such places!), they remain witnesses in a related sense. They must witness the continuity, bloody and baffling as it is, of murder most foul – the powers' continuing havoc against their sisters and brothers. So they question. How could they not?

The question implies a definition of time itself under the hegemony of the Fall, bloodshot through and through – the "meantime" of the powers. Then the "end time," which one concludes is becoming a time native to the sensibility of Daniel.

"How long, how long?" The question encapsulates in a harrowing phrase the unrequited suffering of the innocent through all ages. Time is tolled in the let blood of those slain "for the word of God and the witness they had borne" (Rev. 6:9–11). Time is thus revealed as the blood of Christ and of Christ's own, falling until the end time.

Notable also, and akin to the refusal of Jesus to name "the day or the hour," God here refuses to accord a direct answer to the plaint of the noble slain. Indeed, "that day," "My day," is not to be marked on human calendars or in the stars.

Hardly, be it added in all justice, do the martyrs raise their plaint in order to preempt the mystery. No, it is not this or that date that tears a cry from their throats.

The outcry arises from something akin to this: the honorable passion of those who have died for justice' sake – and would have others spared the same fate. If such things must be, they ask; if evil must win the day, and the year, and the very eon – (and since the murder of the innocent can never be equated with the divine will) – why cannot God turn evil times around? When will the cruel kingdom of necessity collapse in a rubble and the sword fall to rust? When will a new name be conferred on the world?

To feel a like longing – more, to know that such longings, like fires banked in the long night of the tyrants – that such longings outlast death itself, and flare on the lips of the noble dead – is this not to summon and rejoice in the highest understanding of the human itself?

The martyrs, and the "system" that disposed of them. And then the outcry. In El Salvador, for example, new initiatives are currently in the air. The ARENA party that sanctioned, if it did not order, the deaths of Romero and the Jesuits, sits firm in the saddle. NAFTA has arrived on the scene, hiring its cheap un-unionized labor force. And most helpful of all to the new normalizers, a collusive archbishop has been appointed. He has not delayed in making known his version of the new world order. Nor have his chums in ARENA and the army. According to the *National Catholic Reporter,*

> The archbishop of San Salvador's acceptance of the rank of army brigadier general has provoked criticism from some laity and religious in El Salvador, who accuse the archbishop of turning his back on the past. Archbishop Fernando Saenz Lacalle, however had defended his appointment, saying it is something "normal" within the Catholic Church. Eight church leaders including Saenz, were given top military rank by the high command of the Salvadoran armed forces during a private ceremony in late January in the capital. Saenz...was granted the highest rank in the forces; brigadier general... Saenz says that the army has changed its character as part of the peace process...I have no reason to be giving excuses or explanations or asking for forgiveness, since I am merely fulfilling a role stipulated by the church for the well being of (military) souls.

February 21, 1997

In *Apostle of Peace,* Jesuit Jon Sobrino, survivor of the murder of his brothers in San Salvador, writes of a new world order (one thinks, how weirdly like the old one) that finds the noble dead inconvenient:

> I have come to the conclusion that martyrs are an obstacle, and for that reason there hovers over them a great silence which I want to denounce. This silence makes me indignant because it expresses ingratitude – one of the sins to avoid, according to St. Ignatius – and above all because it impoverishes this already destitute civilization. They want to deprive the martyrs of reality, as though they were things of the past, relegated to museums, not of interest to a world that has arrived at the end of history. The silence is notorious in the official realm...Only the poor, this is sure, remember the martyrs with affection. But the most important thing is to discover how the analysts of the sys-

> tem justify this silence. To synthesize, they say that really to remember the martyrs and to make of them our best tradition would bring to the actual moment more bad than good; social traumas, intolerance, aggressiveness, all things that should disappear in the new pragmatic, neoliberal "global village." The reason given for silencing the martyrs is, while unjust, very logical. The martyrs are obstacles and continue to be dangerous. Even after their death, they continue to live. They bring to the light of day the truth about our world today, but they also illuminate how we can build a world on truth, compassion, love, justice…

"The end." Truly much is to come – great days, a final day, events in sum that we humans are helpless to bring about. Thus human limits, incapacities, renegings and shortfalls – these are central to faithful understanding, and to grieving.

That theme of limit and boundary will bear underscoring once more. No human power or political system, no matter how benign, enlightened, compassionate, or farseeing, can bear the weight or repute of naming itself (or being named) the final form of things, the form of the "end time." Nor can the most benign of such arrangements as might be brought into being, however unlikely a happening. Such an achievement cannot preempt *Pleroma* – the restoration, healing, unity, joy, the avatar, the luster and allure of that Day.

We wait. The Day will descend, like heavenly Jerusalem, "from on high" (Rev. 21:10), an act of God. An act beyond human powers, comparable in the end time to the act of creation in the beginning. We await the end, too, of the outcry of the martyrs, their freeing from the pain of our world, the toils of time, the empery of death. The ensuing rapture, the kiss of Christ on their lips. A new cry, filling the air of the new creation: Alleluia!

Perhaps most wondrous of all, we await the clairvoyant judgment of Christ, the setting-in-balance of the perennially tipsy scales of the systems of worldly "justice." We await all this. The end – an act of God and of no other.

Meantime (all time is a meantime with respect to the sovereign end time) we take our cue from the martyrs. We endure, summoning what contentment we can muster, the sorry approximations, inflations, and imitations in the structure and authority of church and state. We proceed with the tasks we are called to, eyes fixed on the prize, hearts more or less steady, awaiting God's hour.

Angels, we are told, surround and abide with us. About us, hints and voices tell of the task to be done, the way to be followed. Our vocation: persevering in modest work, in accord with God's design. Thus offering hope to others, lending substance to the "meantime." In an orbit of love, ringed about with the spirits, we labor and dance, mourn and rejoice, dwelling in the temperate (or torrid – but in any case twilit) zone of God's delay.

Daniel 8:15 A strange form of consolation here. Daniel the seer, whose wisdom may be thought greatly to surpass our own, stands in perplexity, stalemated. The meaning of the incursive animals, as well as of the angelic dialogue, escape him entirely. What can it all mean?

Daniel 8:16 A voice summons Gabriel, the first of the angels named, to stand with the seer as helpmeet. Angels, we are reminded once more, abound in our bible, Jewish and Christian alike. We turn a page, and the visage of some mighty spirit meets our gaze. In Malachi 3:1, an "angel of the covenant" is spoken of. Later, in Daniel, Michael is singled out as "your prince" (Dan. 10:21); and again, as the "great prince who has charge of your people" (Dan. 12:1).

These angels may be thought of as spirits of access; with a strong arm they open wide the dense, all but impenetrable thicket of time and this world. And beware: for every angel, a dark "other" exists, a spirit of a far different order, a harbinger of woe. Behind the wall that would hem us in, unaccountable and arrogant, guarding the realm of death, lurk the dynasts *(archoi),* the principalities. Clamorous and spurious both, they ape the spirits of God even as they oversee and govern the systems of this world. In this they are skilled indeed, buttressing, energizing, justifying, and rendering plausible the fallen creation, the structures given over to death. But these dark spirits hardly go unchallenged. Great angels, stand with us!

The end time, according to the mighty angel, is here anticipated in the downfall of tyrants. And in less spectacular fashion, now and again we, too, take note of a breakthrough. The saints, enlightened by angels of access, summon the powers to judgment. (Thus the reversal of fortune that occurs in courtrooms when peacemakers, themselves summoned as criminals, calmly indict the powers, the judges and prosecutors.) Let it be recorded gratefully that such events are occurring in many places, to the chagrin of public authority, of war makers and keepers of abortion clinics and death rows, those dark guardians of lawless law and disorderly order.

Thus we underscore too the import of challenges to the high and mighty. In the courtrooms of the principalities, defendants are transformed; they take heart, grow burningly eloquent, summon the great angels to their side. Thus they (we) anticipate the final day, literally re-minding the powers and the public (and the church!) of the sovereignty of God above every principality. They double the heart's might – persevering as they do in truth telling in a time of woe.

Daniel 8:18 ff. The end time is also the time of the "wrath of God," of God's indignation and anger. "The anger of God is directed primarily against the priesthood" (Anderson). As in the past, Isaiah warned his people that Assyria had become the "rod of God's anger," so now Antiochus arises to purify and rebuke the faithless. A number of priests turn renegade and join him, both covertly and openly. There follows a shocking degradation of holy offices, as even certain among the high priests become surrogate persecutors of their own. Indeed, the profligate betrayer Jason becomes a type – the betrayer of a holy office (2 Macc. 4:7–26).

As to our own day or Daniel's, a question arises: can a faith that knows no anger be called faithful to the God who from time to time erupts in anger? And further: against what is God's anger directed today? What is its source? What is one to make of a church of no anger? Deep matters! Justice outraged, justice unrestored. Or – no consolation – justice delayed indefinitely. And justice is surely never restored by a church of no anger.

Justice unrestored. If it knows nothing of anger in face of an unjust world, the church itself must be indicted as unjust. Worse, the church itself often persecutes and silences those who dare summon it to judgment and justice. What godliness can such a church presume to, before a benighted world; what light can it bear, what nourishment of mind and spirit? If we cannot keep our own house as a humane dwelling, its door open to seekers, its inhabitants serene, valiant, compassionate – what godliness remains in us? So often the excluded must turn away, seeking elsewhere the spirit and practice of Christ.

A further question arises (though almost never officially). What may be thought to befall the community that distorts the message and example of the Savior? One can speak only of a bargain concluded, an assimilation to the world, whose stigmata are these: racism, sexism, homophobia, violence, exclusion.

The world offers a hearty welcome, an open door, many emoluments, to such a church. Welcome to the world of chagrin, of conformity, of moral futility, of a gospel effectively silenced.

To speak of the principalities, one notes this also: they require no better servant than this or that grand inquisitor. Obsessive, lacerating, he sums up the passions of other civil servants of darkness – judges, prosecutors, keepers, torturers, executioners. With this difference, which is possibly the whole matter, he has made crime into a pseudo-epiphany of the holy. Murder, according to him, is a matter of God's will. Even the murder of Christ?

Let us walk softly here. Let us suggest this: according to this grand eminence, Christ has been surpassed. And to put matters plain, the Holy One is surpassed by the speaker. How describe him, this malicious logician, this infinitely persuasive ecclesiastic, his ear to the ground of history (a certain kind of history, to be sure), a latter-day high priest or judge with secular credentials; a Jason, a Menelaus, a Caiphas, Annas, Herod, Pilate? In this acolyte of the principalities, conspire (doubling the damage wrought by each) the twin powers of church and state – this anti-prophet, a damning witness for the prosecution.

Through this one, and with him and in him, the church is invited – nay, urged – to come on a better way. Better? Feckless, servile, calamitous as that way has shown itself? A way that throughout history has led its besotted votaries nowhere? A way along which the chariots have tossed aside or ridden under the holy ones; destroyed them as useless, fruitless, or worse – as impediments to imperial designs? Better than the way of Christ? The kenotic way – the way of suffering, weakness, and indignity – the self-emptying of God?

Daniel 8:23–25 And those generations of rulers, what of them? Crowning the criminal line, we arrive at one who surpasses all others in wickedness. Survivor as he is, Daniel is haunted by the nightmarish memory of Antiochus. When will the prophet rid himself of this haunt? Daniel must concede much to his dark genius; Antiochus "succeeds in all he puts hand to." He raises betrayal to high art. A gorgon, he battens on the destruction of others. He takes by surprise and overcomes the virtuous and unwary, even the faithful. All are scrutinized in view of loyalty to himself. And no one found wanting is spared.

Less crafty (or even equally so), his adversaries fall like a harvest to the blade of the hooded one. And then – he overreaches himself. In ways unspecified (perhaps already specified, perhaps the crimes already recounted are the point), Antiochus declares war against "the Prince of Princes." And at that juncture, he falls – from grace, from power, from life itself. We are not told the occasion of his fall. And yet by inference we are told. "No hand is raised against him." The mystery of the tyrant's passing can be conveyed only in an image (useful before, in Daniel's interpretation of a former tyrant's dream). It was the living rock, fashioned by no human hand, that destroyed the overweening statue of the king (Dan. 2:34).

That nefarious statue will be recalled. Cruelly exact, towering above, it mirrored darkly the pride of its royal model. Purportedly it was an image of largesse; it bestowed on mere humans a preternatural surfeit. Or turned a dark brow on dissidents. Exacting a spurious divine tribute, it quelled all – save Daniel and his faithful friends.

And yet the portent proved unstable, foolishly vulnerable. A mysterious rock moved against it; vain as the image was, it could not stand. So the rock, a living being, disposed of the effrontery. Then the rock grew and filled the earth. Thy kingdom come.

1 Maccabees 6:7 ff. is more forthright, literal. Antiochus dies of "chagrin." It is an illustration – a massively arrogant spirit is unable (like the great statue in the dream) to sustain itself. Deadly depression follows. His military adventuring has gone nowhere; likewise the abominations he worked against the Jews of Jerusalem. The image of Zeus erected in the temple is pulled down; the temple is purified and renewed. Alas, even the glory of death on a battlefield escapes Antiochus. Enfeebled, he dies in his bed in a foreign land. *Sic transit tyrannus.**

Daniel 8:26 Daniel is instructed to "seal the vision of evenings and mornings" whose truth is here attested to. He will

* *Sic transit tyrannus* – "So passes the tyrant."

be similarly instructed later (Dan. 12:4). His present visions, as has been indicated, are all of endings and new beginnings (the beginnings are only purportedly new: though the faces differ, the sword is unsheathed again and again). The cycle of royal terror is unbroken. The kings know no different behavior; they are ignorant of any history other than that of their predecessors. Brute force and bare fact swamp the imagination; forbidding edicts follow, which permit no competing vision of human life, no critique of the slavish culture they preside over. And by implication, their subjects, chattels, and victims are forbidden any history of their own. Prophecy? It is illegal, punishable.

Enter Daniel. Legal, illegal, what matter to him? He is privy to a far different tradition than that of the tyrants. Let prophecy roll like a torrent! He dares all; the mighty shall tumble down, the lowly be vindicated.

The timing of the mighty event, the Day of reckoning, is unknown, and remains so to this day. By strict design of God. The act of God inaugurating God's realm is beyond all human reckoning. And yet it "will be," and this within time.

Daniel assumes yet another guise; this one is lofty, dreamlike. In these episodes he seems to live half in, half out of time and this world. Ironies abound, conveyed in word and silence. Disclosure is followed by denial of disclosure. An angelic finger lies upon his lips, then withdraws. It is as though the hand of an angel is near, loosing, then sealing his tongue. What has he seen? Whatever, whoever – nothing of it must be told.

In light of these episodes, Daniel must be accounted the humiliated servant of the secret of the end time. In silence and withholding he serves the divine freedom, the inviolable Promise. And he points our vocation in the same direction. We also are so to serve, and thereby as keepers of the Promise (often in silence and rejection) are to be liberated from time and its tyrants.

Daniel 8:27 The guardian Daniel keeps the word. But the word is dazzling, even appalling. To preserve such a secret is a burden that overwhelms. Daniel undergoes a trauma (surely an endearing touch, given the formidable persona of earlier episodes). For its splendor and terror, the secret all but breaks his bones.

And yet he breathes deep, and finds a measure of calm. Once more, we are told, he goes about the king's business. He knows something that the king, come hell or high water (each is a prospect), will never know.

The Borrowing and Lending of Prophecy

The Book of Daniel

9 In the first year of Darius son of Ahasuerus, by birth a Mede,
who became king over the realm of the Chaldeans – 2in the
first year of his reign, I, Daniel, perceived in the books the number
of years that, according to the word of the Lord to the prophet
Jeremiah, must be fulfilled for the devastation of Jerusalem,
namely, seventy years.

3Then I turned to the Lord God, to seek an answer by prayer and
supplication with fasting and sackcloth and ashes.

4I prayed to the Lord my God and made confession, saying, "Ah,
Lord, great and awesome God, keeping covenant and steadfast love
with those who love you and keep your commandments, 5we have
sinned and done wrong, acted wickedly and rebelled, turning aside
from your commandments and ordinances. 6We have not listened
to your servants the prophets, who spoke in your name to our
kings, our princes, and our ancestors, and to all the people of the
land.

7"Righteousness is on your side, O Lord, but open shame, as at
this day, falls on us, the people of Judah, the inhabitants of Jerusalem, and all Israel, those who are near and those who are far away,
in all the lands to which you have driven them, because of the
treachery that they have committed against you. 8Open shame, O
Lord, falls on us, our kings, our officials, and our ancestors, because
we have sinned against you. 9To the Lord our God belong mercy
and forgiveness, for we have rebelled against him, 10and have not
obeyed the voice of the Lord our God by following his laws, which
he set before us by his servants the prophets.

11"All Israel has transgressed your law and turned aside, refusing
to obey your voice. So the curse and the oath written in the law of
Moses, the servant of God, have been poured out upon us, because
we have sinned against you. 12He has confirmed his words, which
he spoke against us and against our rulers, by bringing upon us a
calamity so great that what has been done against Jerusalem has
never before been done under the whole heaven. 13Just as it is writ-

ten in the law of Moses, all this calamity has come upon us. We did
not entreat the favor of the Lord our God, turning from our iniquities and reflecting on his fidelity. [14]So the Lord kept watch over this
calamity until he brought it upon us. Indeed, the Lord our God is
right in all that he has done; for we have disobeyed his voice.

[15]"And now, O Lord our God, who brought your people out of
the land of Egypt with a mighty hand and made your name renowned even to this day – we have sinned, we have done wickedly.
[16]O Lord, in view of all your righteous acts, let your anger and
wrath, we pray, turn away from your city Jerusalem, your holy
mountain; because of our sins and the iniquities of our ancestors,
Jerusalem and your people have become a disgrace among all our
neighbors. [17]Now therefore, O our God, listen to the prayer of
your servant and to his supplication, and for your own sake, Lord,
let your face shine upon your desolated sanctuary. [18]Incline your
ear, O my God, and hear. Open your eyes and look at our desolation and the city that bears your name. We do not present our supplication before you on the ground of our righteousness, but on the
ground of your great mercies. [19]O Lord, hear; O Lord, forgive; O
Lord, listen and act and do not delay! For your own sake, O my
God, because your city and your people bear your name!"

[20]While I was speaking, and was praying and confessing my sin
and the sin of my people Israel, and presenting my supplication
before the Lord my God on behalf of the holy mountain of my
God – [21]while I was speaking in prayer, the man Gabriel, whom I
had seen before in a vision, came to me in swift flight at the time of
the evening sacrifice. [22]He came and said to me, "Daniel, I have
now come out to give you wisdom and understanding. [23]At the
beginning of your supplications a word went out, and I have come
to declare it, for you are greatly beloved. So consider the word and
understand the vision:

[24]"Seventy weeks are decreed for your people and your holy city:
to finish the transgression, to put an end to sin, and to atone for
iniquity, to bring in everlasting righteousness, to seal both vision
and prophet, and to anoint a most holy place. [25]Know therefore

and understand: from the time that the word went out to restore and rebuild Jerusalem until the time of an anointed prince, there shall be seven weeks; and for sixty-two weeks it shall be built again with streets and moat, but in a troubled time. 26After the sixty-two weeks, an anointed one shall be cut off and shall have nothing, and the troops of the prince who is to come shall destroy the city and the sanctuary. Its end shall come with a flood, and to the end there shall be war. Desolations are decreed. 27He shall make a strong covenant with many for one week, and for half of the week he shall make sacrifice and offering cease; and in their place shall be an abomination that desolates, until the decreed end is poured out upon the desolator."

The Borrowing and Lending of Prophecy

Daniel 9 The preceding chapter included both a vision and its interpretation. Here we have a different structure, a borrowing by Daniel from the older prophetic scripture, especially from the book of Jeremiah. Following that comes a lengthy prayer and an angelic (and closely veiled) interpretation of the older prophet. (We recall that at the time of Daniel, 200 BCE, earlier prophetic books, including Jeremiah, had only an informal, not yet canonical, status.)

A wonderful continuity, as prophet borrows from prophet, deep calling to deep. How wise of Daniel! Stalemated, he proceeds to "consult the books," seeking light on his own horrific lifetime. We have taken note of his stalemate, staggered as he is by the charge laid on him; the secrets of the end time, and he their appointed guardian. Like one at the end of all resource, he turns to the tradition, seeking a word of hope or reassurance. Is there not an ancient message that, called forth in midrash, may shed light on his bewilderment?

He opens the scroll, seeking a word of reassurance, even of consolation. Midrash, constantly at work, constantly breathing life on the ancient revelations. A work of faith, an open eye. Does not the process go back and back? Was not each of the prophets charged to speak the ancient word anew? Did not each shed a measure of light on the darkness of this or that time – prophetic times being invariably dark?

Amid great darkness, Daniel opens the scroll. Thus once more an important principle is illustrated. This: while time lasts, scripture is never to be thought, or dealt with, as lying inert on a page. No, it is "charged with the grandeur of God," a prodigious energy. It flares up in our face; it brings to bear upon our sorry human scene the very truth of God. The Word is light and ardor, darkness and reproof. Fiery, icy, comforting, reproving, disconcerting, cutting asunder, "striking to the joining place of bone and marrow," it works a strange surgery of the spirit.

If the seed is to fall on good ground, it must wait on an open heart. Open like loosened soil to the rain, we imagine the world anew, with a courage to match the ancient heroes of the Word. And so gifted we embrace and embody that new world, showing its presence in love for one another. And in the confounding of the powers. The Word waits on a Daniel.

Who, here and now, shall ponder Abraham, Moses, Esther, Jeremiah? Who shall show once more that a prophet is in our midst? Let that one summon the Word, place it firmly against a new situation, then (daringly, if so must be) apply it, like a poultice to a suppurating wound. Let it work, whether in cherishing the victimized and the oppressed, or in confronting the mighty by speaking truth to power. (We have seen such a renewed sense of the Word, in this very book – Dan. 9:24 ff.; 11:35; 12:3).

Here we see a change of focus; Daniel's conscience touches on home ground. He has no more to say concerning the crimes of the king, whose malice previously seized upon the intransigent servitor in an explosion of horror. Now Daniel's eyes lights on a different prey. He proceeds to utter a scorching judgment laid against the sins of his own people.

It cannot be said too often (the prophets never tire of repeating it): the judgment of God in no wise exempts, overlooks, makes plausible or of small account the sins of a covenanted people.

This is simply a biblical truism, verified again and again.

Indeed, the catastrophes surrounding the age of prophecy, the destruction of the temple and the holy city, together with the exile – these are not primarily paid to arbitrary fits and starts of tyrants (though they are also that, of course). They are primarily judgments as a consequence of socialized sin, and covenantal violations.

Our own sins bring down the heavens? Such a word strikes hard, then as now. The consequence of our sins? The peremptory catastrophes befall; they ill befit the "self image" of the self-justified.

We have heard it in our day: deceptive, pseudo-religious talk of us Americans as inhabiting (indeed creating!) something known as the "kingdom of light"; and the adversary wickedly reigning in his "kingdom of evil." Let it be said once for all: such twisting of a moral situation to our own advantage is blasphemous, anti-biblical.

Daniel's judgment against his own – how praise such courage and perspicacity? We are surprised once more; the judgment takes the unexpected form of a prayer. The prayer issues from his sense of who "I" and "we" are before God.

God help us, in sum. He sees sin as infecting first of all, in most dire fashion, his own community. It is there, if anywhere, that reconciling must begin.

Be this noted, too: the prayer of Daniel, the admission of communal guilt, the supplicating of forgiveness are entirely proper to believers. (Even if such prayer is judged by the culture at large to be irrelevant or stupid.)

And yet, despite the biblical urgings, how rarely such prayers are uttered in Christian congregations! Passionless! If uttered at all, how often reduced to a matter of rot and rote, having little or no bearing on repentance, on the sin that pollutes our days – Christian complicity with the war-making empire, blighted moral vision, inertia, and woeful neutrality.

*Dignum et justum,** Daniel's plea is that the reconciling grace of God bring us to a better heart. In contrast, secular methods of righting wrongs are plain and predictable, in little need of elaboration here. We see in the world an endless round of confrontation, accusation, public outcry; vendettas, suits for recovery of damages, denunciations and condemnations, taking of matters into one's own hands, jailings – even the domestic body count left by capital punishment.

Not to speak of internecine killings, wars, and rumors of war. Not to omit abortion mills, euthanasia on demand, and medicos ready and willing to rid the human scene of the unwanted or unproductive. In a culture like ours, the ills of the world are addressed violently, with fire and sword, scalpel, a pull of the switch. By such means, useless as they are, wicked, worldly systems actually announce that they seek reform and mitigation of ills!

Thus too is dismissed, often with contempt, the admission of one's own guilt (or of communal guilt), or a search for the strong relief of reconciliation amid conflict. Of what remote usefulness, according to the world, is such self flagellation, the undermining of a sense of worth, of ego vindicated, the relief offered by actions bloody, bold, and resolute?

And the affair known as faith, what of that? According to the world, faith seeks the approval of a highly problematic being named God. Thus the critique is developed: faith, a recourse to magic, to a human construct of the all but unknowable (if not the nonexistent). A god who is no more than a surrogate, truth told, for moral lassitude and fear of reality.

**Dignum et justum* – "worthily and fittingly."

One notes here the convenient ignoring of the "other side" of faith, exemplified admirably in Daniel and his community: courage, a lion's den endured, a fiery furnace quenched. On the world's terms as well, such images are admirable, bespeaking as they do courage and moral consistency. But they are ignored; they merit no attention.

The scandal of faith is inwardness. The scandal is encountering the world on its own terms, in its own courts and jails – and overcoming. And not by force of arms. The scandal is double: a nonviolent God, and human godliness.

The lengthy prayer of Daniel is spoken; indeed, its tone were better understood not as a calm, measured speech, but as an outcry. We have a drama of naked truth. A reassuring contrast is also implied. When earlier an angel spoke, Daniel trembled in all his being and fainted away. Here we witness no such trauma; the mood is one of assurance and mutuality.

The prayer is also wonderfully dramatic. God is witness to the struggle of the people (personified as it is, brought to pitch in the valiance of their spiritual mentor). But this is our interpretation: of his pivotal role, Daniel says nothing. His prayer is effortful, wrenching. He struggles with the Holy One, cries aloud, fasts and mourns. A sense of his people! Above all, he would restore an integrity long since insulted and frittered away.

He knows it in his bones and grieves, this "man of desires." Behold the people. They have all but lost a sense of God. They are pummeled like an unrisen dough into the leaven of the nations, enslaved and humiliated. And worse. In the loss of tradition, they have been spiritually dismembered, dry bones in a desert place. Once a community of rich tradition, but no longer! What now, empty of hand and heart, can they offer the tormented world? Worship no longer instructs them as to their vocation, harsh, inevitably tragic, and despite all, crucial *vis à vis* the liberation of the dwellers of earth.

Let the sorrowful matter be put simply. The exiles are all but assimilated. Like the ancestors, the slaves in Egypt, they are resigned to the status assigned them (status in place of vocation!), thrust at them – not by God, but by a succession of tyrants. The kings have created slaves, and created them twice over. First by decree, then by the victims' bowing to the decree. The prior vision of life in God and one another, of an honorable covenant, is radically altered. The masters have created and imposed an image of ineluctable destiny. And the people bow their necks before the yoke – perpetual exile, enslavement. No help for it, no Moses, no exodus. In this dolorous state, an alternate sense of themselves, of a lofty vocation, of "being sent" to the nations – these have all but vanished.

Here the pain, the loss, the inner brokenness. They no longer account themselves a saving sign. They ignore and contemn their own prophets. In consequence, little of faith or trust remains in the God who, as they once confessed, saves. Adrift in a stagnant sea of powerlessness, the ark of salvation is stalemated, "a painted ship upon a painted ocean." The social fabric is rotted away. No wonder, one thinks, that a monstrous image of Zeus towers and glowers in their midst. It is a sign, a shadow upon the soul of the culture.

What the prayer of Daniel omits is important also. There is no petition for divine vengeance, nothing of spleen, no longing for retribution, no denouncing or listing the crimes of Archelaus – this though the tyrant stands as one of the cruelest in history.

Daniel 9:5 Not the crimes of Archelaus but our own must be recalled, if ever these are to be renounced. So we have an exhaustive catalogue of the transgressions of the people, as well as access to God, disconcerting, trembling, fearful. "We" (underscored!) "have sinned," "done wrong," "acted wickedly," "turned aside," "rebelled."

Conventional piety would approach the deity in an entirely different mood: a position of strength, a sound basis of *quid pro quo,* of bargaining and self justification. We have in contrast to the prayer of Daniel a classical pharisaic prayer (by no means a matter done with!). The latter prayer is addressed, truth told, by the Pharisee to himself. His words reek; through he purports to address a deity, he has no need of such a being. He has need only of himself, self approved, self justifying. The prayer is no prayer at all; it is a classic example, rather, of a non-prayer, of how not to pray.

Or if we allow this eloquent monologue the term "prayer," it is surely an ambiguous one. It addresses a mirror image, a god who presumably approves the one who approves the god. Approves the god for his admirable creation of the Pharisee, who consoles himself with a full catalogue of pharisaic good works (in contrast, of course, to the ill works of the publican). The Pharisee astonishes with his meticulous detail; not a virtue is passed over, his "head unbowed."

Clearly (to all but himself) he is a lapsarian, a strict reformer of evil mores (in others). He takes a dim view of us humans. "I give thanks, O God, that I am not as others; grasping, crooked, adulterous (or even like this tax collector). No, I fast twice a week, I tithe on all I possess..." (Luke 18:9 ff.) The stance, the language place us in earshot of a perennial phenomenon. We too have heard (perhaps we have uttered?) such hollow orotund phrases; in effect, I am my own god.

Prophetic prayer ignores the clamorous ego. In place of self congratulation, the words of Daniel provide a merciless catalogue of the shortcomings of the people – his own people – and by extension, his own sins. Its implication bears repeating. This: the judgment of God lies heavy upon the "people of God"(or those who so designate themselves). In consequence let them (let us) tread warily, indulging in no large claims. Mayhap religious phrases roll too lightly from our lips?

A Pharisee in our midst (a Pharisee in our heart) is not to be let off easily. Let him know that he has missed the mark. Far different matters than those he so exquisitely dwells on are really in question: matters such as justice, compassion, and love.

Daniel 9:6 The prayer of Daniel is further evidence of his status as prophet. He utters the truth of a common predicament. All, high and low, have turned a stony ear to the word of God: "kings, princes, ancestors, people;" likewise "those who are near and those afar, in the lands to which you have driven them." The indictment is devastating, a prelude to Paul's flat statement in his letter to the Romans, chapters 1–3.

Let Daniel indict his own; Paul will indict the entire race (himself included, as he well knew). No one, no generation, no "chosen" of whatever time or place, is exempt from the common plight. "It is as scripture says (Ps. 14:1 ff.); there is no just one, not even one…no one in search of God…Not one of them acts uprightly, no, not one."

To be human is to be needy. And our need, moral void, our helplessness to overcome these lies beyond human capacity, whether for redress or relief. The acknowledgment of our plight is the beginning of wisdom: "All have sinned and fallen short of the glory of God."

Daniel 9:12 What a staggering connection Daniel draws! Who can bear it? Even Jeremiah did not live to see a catastrophe to match this. In the eyes of Daniel the autonomy of God is vindicated, since the "great calamity" has befallen. The temple is a shell and worse; it is fallen, it is an indistinguishable heap amid the rubble of history.

But let us go back in time. Long before the advent of the barbarians, the shell resonated with the cacophony of idolatrous worship. Thus, before the fact, before invasion, seizure, destruction, the tyrant prevailed. And the catastrophe that followed, in a cruelly exact sense, befitted. In a public drama of willful destruction, the true character of the "worship" that preceded is mimed and unmasked. Behold priesthood and people, priding themselves as covenantal, chosen – God's own in ultimate possession of truth! And all was sham.

The worship of Zeus in the holy precinct thus becomes a kind of theater of the absurd, a mocking parody of the worship of unbelieving believers. Generations had assembled in worship of true God; so went the blind rhetoric, the voice of blinded hearts. And they turned away from God to works of injustice and betrayal.

Daniel 9:13 "As it is written." The phrase places a holy seal on the line of prophets, from Jeremiah to our Daniel – and, one thinks as well, forward to Jesus and the Christian testament. Jesus, with his skill at midrash, will borrow the same solemn phrase. Thus the words of the speaker, hearkening back to law and prophets, are enforced, underscored, applied anew, crowning an immemorial tradition. The teaching carries the ancient weight, a weight of glory. It is thus attested anew, as of God – irrefutably holy.

We cannot but note it. The prayer attempts no false justification, no excusing or sidestepping. It says: we must hold the mirror before our face, no matter the shame. Like an Ezekiel, Daniel rattles the dry bones of the nation with words of terror and truth. "Now hear the Word of the Lord!" Acknowledge it at last, the truth! Each and all, we have merited the worst that has befallen.

It comes to this, as he knows – the truth is an only hope. Counter to despair, evasion, dread of the living word, prevarication and pride, the spirit may still breathe life into the dead. Shall rebirth be granted? Yes, for God is God. But first must come admission, the truth of our condition. "We" (not the tyrant; he is but the blind instrument of God's wrath) – *we* are dead. At a dead end. Dead to God's word, dead to compassion and justice.

Dead as we are, nonetheless through a mime and mockery of worship. We dared approach the living God; and this in the house of the dead. In reality, our worship paid tribute and fealty to idols. We differ not a whit from the pagans we affect to despise.

The people have touched bottom. Sinful as we are, despoiled, in mourning, in bondage to a cruel despot – despite all (because of all), hear us!

When all is lost, what may be thought to remain? The people are naked before God and the elements of this world. Naked. But that is not all. They stand naked "before God." Therefore all is not lost. Indeed, it could be argued that much has been gained. (As to what was lost, the detritus were best cast aside in any case; the stupor and spleen and pride of life that brought catastrophe).

Does not truthful prayer on the lips of a suffering prophet imply its favorable hearing? Let us venture this, a noble irony. Taking in account both aura and author, the prayer includes the blessing it sought. The answer is sealed in the envelope. The message is in the medium.

The prayer is like a prostration too. It concedes that God is God, the One who responds to no magical nudging or stroking, who acts solely out of holiness, goodness, and mercy. Will the community welcome the truth it once neglected and despised? At long last, we shall. Where death was in command, life has prevailed. Let God's favor rest once more on the desolate sanctuary, that larger form and image of the heart.

Daniel 9:15–19 Thus Daniel bestirs the memory of the tribe, recalling the history of crime and consequence. The climax of the prayer is distilled in a few words, brief but incomparably beautiful. "O Lord, hear; O Lord, forgive; O Lord, take heed and act, for your city and your people are named for you." No more trafficking in false gods, in untruth and self inflation! The people, chastised and cleansed, take heart, speak in the person of Daniel, "the greatly beloved."

Daniel 9:20 After this noble interlude the main theme is resumed: the summoning of the words of Jeremiah, his light cast on contemporary event. The prayer of Jeremiah was uttered, as Daniel reports, "at the time of the evening sacrifice." The tyrant has forbidden the rite, but he cannot stifle the faith that bursts forth, as though from a sealed tomb. It is a major theme recalled by implication and conveyed in a subtle code: illegitimate power is rendered null and void before God.

Daniel 9:21 Gabriel is Daniel's guardian angel. From the opening syllable of Daniel's prayer, he was summoned to stand at the side of God's servant. And even as it was uttered, the prayer was heard.

The message of Gabriel has been called the key to this chapter, indeed to the entire book. Dare we take the key in hand and turn it, to seek what lies beyond? Pondering the fate of his people under Antiochus, Daniel's attention is drawn to two passages of Jeremiah: 25:11–14, and 29:10–14. Each of these has announced an exile of seventy years. But now, a correction. It is offered through an angel to a later prophet, one endowed with an authority equal to that of Jeremiah. This: the time of testing is to be extended, to a time all but beyond calculating – "seventy weeks of years."

In effect, scripture is being written anew at the behest of God's messenger. Daniel is made the vessel of fresh inspiration. Thus too Daniel renews the question which faith never ceases to raise: How long, O Lord?

My brother and our friends were summoned to trial in Portland, Maine in early 1997. Their crime: an Isaiahan interference with a naval vessel, a ship capable for the first time in history of waging atomic, biological, and chemical warfare. Which is to say, an instrument of terror and extermination, presuming to arrogate to human hands the "last day" of Daniel's vision. "Until the end, there shall be war, the desolation that is decreed."

Months later the accused were found guilty – of pronouncing government authorities guilty of high crime. They were sentenced and rigorously punished. Indeed, they are still being punished. And we too raise the cry: How long, O Lord?

Daniel, Sent

The Book of Daniel

10 In the third year of King Cyrus of Persia a word was revealed to Daniel, who was named Belteshazzar. The word was true, and it concerned a great conflict. He understood the word, having received understanding in the vision.

2At that time I, Daniel, had been mourning for three weeks. 3I had eaten no rich food, no meat or wine had entered my mouth, and I had not anointed myself at all, for the full three weeks. 4On the twenty-fourth day of the first month, as I was standing on the bank of the great river (that is, the Tigris), 5I looked up and saw a man clothed in linen, with a belt of gold from Uphaz around his waist. 6His body was like beryl, his face like lightning, his eyes like flaming torches, his arms and legs like the gleam of burnished bronze, and the sound of his words like the roar of a multitude. 7I, Daniel, alone saw the vision; the people who were with me did not see the vision, though a great trembling fell upon them, and they fled and hid themselves. 8So I was left alone to see this great vision. My strength left me, and my complexion grew deathly pale, and I retained no strength. 9Then I heard the sound of his words; and when I heard the sound of his words, I fell into a trance, face to the ground.

10But then a hand touched me and roused me to my hands and knees. 11He said to me, "Daniel, greatly beloved, pay attention to the words that I am going to speak to you. Stand on your feet, for I have now been sent to you." So while he was speaking this word to me, I stood up trembling. 12He said to me, "Do not fear, Daniel, for from the first day that you set your mind to gain understanding and to humble yourself before your God, your words have been heard, and I have come because of your words. 13But the prince of the kingdom of Persia opposed me twenty-one days. So Michael, one of the chief princes, came to help me, and I left him there with the prince of the kingdom of Persia, 14and have come to help you understand what is to happen to your people at the end of days. For there is a further vision for those days."

15While he was speaking these words to me, I turned my face toward the ground and was speechless. 16Then one in human form touched my lips, and I opened my mouth to speak, and said to the one who stood before me, "My lord, because of the vision such pains have come upon me that I retain no strength. 17How can my lord's servant talk with my lord? For I am shaking, no strength remains in me, and no breath is left in me."

18Again one in human form touched me and strengthened me. 19He said, "Do not fear, greatly beloved, you are safe. Be strong and courageous!" When he spoke to me, I was strengthened and said, "Let my lord speak, for you have strengthened me." 20Then he said, "Do you know why I have come to you? Now I must return to fight against the prince of Persia, and when I am through with him, the prince of Greece will come. 21But I am to tell you what is inscribed in the book of truth. There is no one with me who contends against these princes except Michael, your prince.

11 As for me, in the first year of Darius the Mede, I stood up to support and strengthen him. 2"Now I will announce the truth to you. Three more kings shall arise in Persia. The fourth shall be far richer than all of them, and when he has become strong through his riches, he shall stir up all against the kingdom of Greece. 3Then a warrior king shall arise, who shall rule with great dominion and take action as he pleases. 4And while still rising in power, his kingdom shall be broken and divided toward the four winds of heaven, but not to his posterity, nor according to the dominion with which he ruled; for his kingdom shall be uprooted and go to others besides these.

5"Then the king of the south shall grow strong, but one of his officers shall grow stronger than he and shall rule a realm greater than his own realm. 6After some years they shall make an alliance, and the daughter of the king of the south shall come to the king of the north to ratify the agreement. But she shall not retain her power, and his offspring shall not endure. She shall be given up, she and her attendants and her child and the one who supported her.

"In those times [7]a branch from her roots shall rise up in his place.
He shall come against the army and enter the fortress of the king of
the north, and he shall take action against them and prevail. [8]Even
their gods, with their idols and with their precious vessels of silver
and gold, he shall carry off to Egypt as spoils of war. For some years
he shall refrain from attacking the king of the north; [9]then the latter shall invade the realm of the king of the south, but will return to
his own land.

[10]"His sons shall wage war and assemble a multitude of great
forces, which shall advance like a flood and pass through, and again
shall carry the war as far as his fortress. [11]Moved with rage, the king
of the south shall go out and do battle against the king of the north,
who shall muster a great multitude, which shall, however, be defeated by his enemy. [12]When the multitude has been carried off, his
heart shall be exalted, and he shall overthrow tens of thousands,
but he shall not prevail. [13]For the king of the north shall again raise
a multitude, larger than the former, and after some years he shall
advance with a great army and abundant supplies.

[14]"In those times many shall rise against the king of the south.
The lawless among your own people shall lift themselves up in order to fulfill the vision, but they shall fail. [15]Then the king of the
north shall come and throw up siegeworks, and take a well-fortified
city. And the forces of the south shall not stand, not even his picked
troops, for there shall be no strength to resist. [16]But he who comes
against him shall take the actions he pleases, and no one shall withstand him. He shall take a position in the beautiful land, and all of
it shall be in his power. [17]He shall set his mind to come with the
strength of his whole kingdom, and he shall bring terms of peace
and perform them. In order to destroy the kingdom, he shall give
him a woman in marriage; but it shall not succeed or be to his
advantage. [18]Afterward he shall turn to the coastlands, and shall
capture many. But a commander shall put an end to his insolence;
indeed, he shall turn his insolence back upon him. [19]Then he shall
turn back toward the fortresses of his own land, but he shall
stumble and fall, and shall not be found.

[20]"Then shall arise in his place one who shall send an official for
the glory of the kingdom; but within a few days he shall be broken,
though not in anger or in battle. [21]In his place shall arise a con-
temptible person on whom royal majesty had not been conferred;
he shall come in without warning and obtain the kingdom through
intrigue. [22]Armies shall be utterly swept away and broken before
him, and the prince of the covenant as well. [23]And after an alliance
is made with him, he shall act deceitfully and become strong with a
small party. [24]Without warning he shall come into the richest parts
of the province and do what none of his predecessors had ever
done, lavishing plunder, spoil, and wealth on them. He shall devise
plans against strongholds, but only for a time. [25]He shall stir up his
power and determination against the king of the south with a great
army, and the king of the south shall wage war with a much greater
and stronger army. But he shall not succeed, for plots shall be devised against him [26]by those who eat of the royal rations. They shall
break him, his army shall be swept away, and many shall fall slain.
[27]The two kings, their minds bent on evil, shall sit at one table and
exchange lies. But it shall not succeed, for there remains an end at
the time appointed. [28]He shall return to his land with great wealth,
but his heart shall be set against the holy covenant. He shall work
his will, and return to his own land.

[29]"At the time appointed he shall return and come into the
south, but this time it shall not be as it was before. [30]For ships of
Kittim shall come against him, and he shall lose heart and withdraw. He shall be enraged and take action against the holy covenant. He shall turn back and pay heed to those who forsake the
holy covenant. [31]Forces sent by him shall occupy and profane the
temple and fortress. They shall abolish the regular burnt offering
and set up the abomination that makes desolate. [32]He shall seduce
with intrigue those who violate the covenant; but the people who
are loyal to their God shall stand firm and take action. [33]The wise
among the people shall give understanding to many; for some days,
however, they shall fall by sword and flame, and suffer captivity and
plunder. [34]When they fall victim, they shall receive a little help, and

many shall join them insincerely. [35]Some of the wise shall fall, so that they may be refined, purified, and cleansed, until the time of the end, for there is still an interval until the time appointed.

[36]"The king shall act as he pleases. He shall exalt himself and consider himself greater than any god, and shall speak horrendous things against the God of gods. He shall prosper until the period of wrath is completed, for what is determined shall be done. [37]He shall pay no respect to the gods of his ancestors, or to the one beloved by women; he shall pay no respect to any other god, for he shall consider himself greater than all. [38]He shall honor the god of fortresses instead of these; a god whom his ancestors did not know he shall honor with gold and silver, with precious stones and costly gifts. [39]He shall deal with the strongest fortresses by the help of a foreign god. Those who acknowledge him he shall make more wealthy, and shall appoint them as rulers over many, and shall distribute the land for a price.

[40]"At the time of the end the king of the south shall attack him. But the king of the north shall rush upon him like a whirlwind, with chariots and horsemen, and with many ships. He shall advance against countries and pass through like a flood. [41]He shall come into the beautiful land, and tens of thousands shall fall victim, but Edom and Moab and the main part of the Ammonites shall escape from his power. [42]He shall stretch out his hand against the countries, and the land of Egypt shall not escape. [43]He shall become ruler of the treasures of gold and of silver, and all the riches of Egypt; and the Libyans and the Ethiopians shall follow in his train. [44]But reports from the east and the north shall alarm him, and he shall go out with great fury to bring ruin and complete destruction to many. [45]He shall pitch his palatial tents between the sea and the beautiful holy mountain. Yet he shall come to his end, with no one to help him.

Daniel, Sent

Daniel 10:1 ff. The final vision unfolds. Its themes are common to Moses, Ezekiel, Jeremiah, Isaiah. Each, we note, received a like gift – unambiguous, dramatic, driving, a kind of Vision To Set One In Motion. Each quaked in his sandals at the prospect, a vocation that opened like the yawn of hell, or the portal of heaven (or both). Each was sent to do justice in a time of injustice, was burdened with a word of truth, costly and unpalatable, to be uttered before tyrants for the sake of an abused people. And, one notes, a word of judgment as well to be uttered to his own people – no excuses stemming from their plight of exile or slavery, no pandering to self pity!

Under such daunting tasks, the prophet stands in dire need of a blessing, an assurance that courage will be granted so that the Word might be uttered in integrity and followed through. We note (after the fact, to be sure) that each, including Daniel, receive such graces – yet for all that are not a whit relieved of fear and trembling. And, need it be added, not a pennyweight is lightened of the charge laid on their shoulders. The terrible word holds steady – a promise, a stark edge: "Speak the truth. I am with you." Daniel thus stands in a great line, and trembles.

Prior to this episode he seems assured and walks steady. We have marveled (and perhaps were somewhat set down?) at his courage, his unquestioning obedience and forthrightness. We saw him uncowed before tyrants, unmasking for all to see the dark underside of power. Assured, steady, he walked the dangerous world. At times, that world became a landscape where death abounded and survival was unlikely – a world that took the form of a furnace stoked or a pride of lions.

Such virtue, such gifts and stature! Was he larger than life? In him were we presented an ideal beyond attaining? Had time and legend rubbed away the rough and left us this icon? We admired, we marveled. And we doubted. He seemed somewhat removed, somewhat rigid, somewhat less (or more?) than human.

Now all is changed. A sea change. Now we can approach him. (A Christian tradition tells how, as an exhausted Jesus came to Calvary, a woman held a towel to his face, wiped away sweat and blood and spittle. Veronica, she of the "true icon," thus won back the face of Christ.) The face of a different Daniel is before us, the face of a suffering servant. He is racked with fear, with second thoughts and physical weakness. He quakes before the great Epiphany. In its wake he undergoes a kind of death. And for this he becomes all the more believable and lovable. A vessel of prejudice, yes, but like any mortal under heaven's thunders, shaking in his flesh and bones.

In previous episodes his riches and variety gleamed from the page: mentor, hero elegant and assured, astute survivor, tamer of lions, defender of the brethren, treading the flames of royal fury, vizard rebuking the fantasies of the mighty. And still a question nagged: what has he undergone of the common plight, the ordinary way? For our part, we are less than we would be, certainly less than we are called to be. Falling short as we do, do we also seek to ferret out in others a shortfall, shortcomings? No unmodified heroes for us, no unqualified greatness! Please – show a hint, an inkling of weakness, dark moods freely confessed! And perhaps our deepest longing of all: let our saints and prophets admit to an onset of fear.

No heroes we, God knows. A voice whispers in our bones: let life unroll an ordinary text, assign us a place in the crowd, a commonsensical anonymity. Let our *lingua franca* be a face-saving "maybe." Up to now, Daniel is pure dazzle. No agony. No Gethsemane. No "strong cry and tears toward the one who could save..." (Heb. 5:7) No "let this cup pass from me..." (Luke 22:42) And then, and then. The greatest of Daniel's visions dawns, sumptuous, premonitory. And the visitation all but breaks his bones. Several times, as we learned, he cries out in protest, recoils, falls to the ground in a faint. And we are strangely consoled. All told, he is one of us, mortal, and bearing the cicatrice of his high calling.

Then the Word is given him. In his laceration of spirit, Daniel is granted the revelation of secrets hidden from the great ancestors. An irony that wounds and heals, both. An act of God, surpassing human incapacity.

Once more Daniel stands upright, uneasy and trembling. And the precious Word rains down. As though to underscore the import of the scene, we note two departures from former literary practice. Belteshazzar, his Babylonian name, stands in the text. Also for the first time in this second section, as it were, in chapters 7–12 – his own account ends. An unnamed witness has set down the record; now Daniel is referred to in the third person. These may be taken as hints. An event of great import, one requiring an independent witness, is to follow.

Daniel 10:2–4 Daniel is discovered mourning, fasting and at prayer. It might be that he is girding himself (and urging a like course on his companions), in view of the punishments soon to befall the tyrant. Or perhaps more to the point, he senses obscurely that a providential moment on behalf of his community impends. In any case we have a Daniel grown dear and familiar. His sense of reality is gentle, sure. He has passed through the fire. Now his hands touch ever so lightly the web of life, and draw thence hints and stirrings as of new birth.

It is as though the music of the spheres sounded in his ear. As though his universe were pregnant with harmonies, requiring only an attentive hand to draw them forth.

He interrupts his day-to-day rhythms, drawing apart (Dan. 10:4). And then the vision appears: a man; or, taking in account the Hebrew numeral offered here, a "single man," a "man alone." (A comparison with Rev. 1:13–16 is rewarding.) The calling of the prophet opens (as in Isa. 6 and Ezek. 1). More accurately, the heavens themselves are sundered. And not a word is spoken. A numinous presence stands before him. A human form is suggested, concentrated, rendered intense by association and likeness; gold, beryl, lightning, flaming torches, burnished bronze, a multitudinous murmur…

Daniel has encountered angels before, but this Being surpasses altogether the angelic nature. Before this Personage he is struck to earth.

No one, we are told elsewhere, has seen God and lived (Exod. 33:20). Daniel's companions have seen nothing, yet the vision ricochets off them too. Something, Someone! Witnessing the sudden transport of their companion, terror seizes them. They take to their heels.

The point here, whether for Daniel or his people, is not the identity of the celestial visitant. (In biblical understanding, the naming of a mystery is forbidden ground. Often as not, naming a visitant is equivalent to laying a claim, objectifying, and thereby nullifying what must remain beyond ken or estimate – a gift.) We are on holy ground. Let us tread softly, and if we seek to know, let us speak only of a godlike epiphany.

There occurs a kind of laying on of hands, an anointing, a credential conferred, an imprimatur, a sending forth – to his people, needy, embattled, encumbered as they are. The moment granted, he and the exiles need never again doubt; providence stands with them. And more. The God who granted this dazzling moment spoke (and will speak again) through such as Daniel.

Daniel 10:10–15 Shortly an angel appears, and an interpretation of the vision is offered. The point is more than enlightenment concerning the impending fall of the tyrant. After all, the death of Antiochus is in the nature of things (the nature of tyranny) quite to be taken for granted. But for Daniel and his people the future is endangered, chancy. As is, alas, always true when the powerful die, the system remains intact. Who shall replace the tyrant? One worse than he? And what shall become of us? A word of hope is our desperate need.

The word is spoken, unequivocally. Then the point of angelic attention shifts. Of final import to the angel of revelation is not the fate of this or that worldly power. Such are ephemeral, redundant. In the world their replacement is easily chosen; there are many aspirants, equally wicked. The Word of God turns elsewhere. That Word must reclaim the death of the just; an event signaling, despite all appearances to the contrary, the victory of grace (Dan. 12:2–3).

Daniel has fallen prone. Then it is as though a sublime ballet were underway. First the angel lifts him to hands and knees; finally he gains strength to stand upright.

An apocalyptic note is struck. Gabriel and Michael, we are told, are angelic warriors engaged in heavenly warfare. We have seen it before. According to the celestial imagery evoked here (and in the Book of Revelation), no earthly war can be purely earthbound. The clash of arms penetrates the heavenly court; God is the prey – the God of peace, and God's peaceable disciples. Scripture harps on the truth.

In view of past and present horrors, and in light of scripture, we can do no less. Let us spell it out again, as warmongering, whether secular and sacred, infects the ages, up to this bristling, murderous moment. Thus. No matter its nature or provocation or slogans or ideology or moral justification, war is above all else a spiritual reality, a close drama of the Fall whose last act aims at the vindication and victory of the principality named Death. Which is to say, war is always and everywhere and chiefly a demonic assault on the God of peace, the Lover of creation. It is an assault on creation itself. As such, war is witnessed and judged by God. Would that the church understood this, and so spoke, in accord with God's Word!

Once more Daniel's soul is all but torn from his body. Has he not already heard and seen things kept secret from the beginning? And yet, all but beyond bearing, more is to come (Dan. 10:14), a "new vision." It is all too much, too quick. Daniel is stricken, in dread of hearing more.

A costly hope is held out to him. Only through endurance, he is told, will the tribulation be overcome. The angel offers the only comfort worth the name: the comfort of renewed strength. Daniel is assured repeatedly that he is greatly loved, that he is a "man of desires." Such praise, falling on a beleaguered servant! Heartened, he girds himself for the awful events that impend.

(Much of this episode can be summarily dealt with, as it is not to our immediate point. There are, however, sublime relics to be attended to, as in the linkage of Dan. 11:1 with Dan. 10:21. The "strengthening" is not for Darius, but for Michael, the heavenly companion of Gabriel.)

Daniel 11:14 Factions, we are told, have arisen among the chosen. When the scroll named for Daniel reached the form that lies in our hands, divisions had hardened. Some among the Jews had been taken hostage in Egypt; others joined the invading armies as mercenaries. Interestingly, the factions are fairly represented by the author of Daniel and Maccabees, as well as by the author of Ecclesiastes, who among other differences includes Simon the Just among those worthy of praise (Eccles. 50:1 ff.).

Daniel 11:21–39 The arch-villain Antiochus enters the scene; he will stand for a time at center stage, inflicting unspeakable suffering on the just. Through him the faith comes under horrific attack; including, as we have seen, three years of blasphemous intrusion upon the precincts of the temple, in the course of which he presided over the "abomination of desolation." A space sacred above all others was given over to worship of Zeus. (The awful episode is recounted also in 1 Macc. 1:54.)

Daniel 11:32 We are told that some among the covenanted learned to adjust – even to this. And in 1 Maccabees, we have this admission: "Many of the people, those who abandoned the Law, joined them [the pagans] and committed evil in the land" (1 Macc. 1:52). And six centuries previous to our text, Hosea spoke in like manner of those who "showed neither faithfulness nor compassion, and no knowledge of God…in the land" (Hos. 4:1).

Daniel 11:33 Then a saving contrast appears. We are introduced to the "wise" (*Hammaskilim,* often identified historically with the later *Hasidim*). They were held in honor among the people; they imparted wisdom, stood firm, and took action against the persecutor. Their resistance was costly; it resulted in many among them "falling by sword and flame, by captivity and plunder."

Thus the "wise" join the company of ancient mentors, martyrs, suffering servants, and saints among whom our Daniel is surely to be honored. They are also (and not solely by word) the teachers of the *Harrakim,* the "many." These also are among the holy. They transmit the lore of the tribe, and their great virtue is courage. They will die, when required, for sake of the holy tradition.

Implacable adversaries of cultural adjustment, the *Hammaskilim* refuse all attempts at assimilation. A comparison with the martyrs of the Maccabean history is inviting. One among these is the high priest Onias, a figure of rare courage. He confronts the king's men, prays for the persecutor, converts him (2 Macc. 3:22–36), and eventually dies at the hands of a renegade viceroy (2 Macc.4:30–34). In another precious hagiography, a mother and her seven sons perish together. Their story becomes a classic among Christians as well as Jews (2 Macc. 7). A renowned elder, Elezear, undoubtedly one of the *Hammaskilim,* also is executed for his fidelity to the Law (2 Macc.6:18–31). Inevitably these heroes bring to mind Daniel and his companions. And could these heroes, one and all, not all be thought forerunners of the Christian martyrs? The early church thought so, and so honored them.

Verse 33 is of great import; it could be taken (along with Dan. 12:3) as a commentary on Isaiah 52:13 to 53:12, the "fourth song of the suffering servant."

Daniel 11:36–39 Three years after he received the crown, Antiochus took to himself the title Epiphanes, "the god manifest." He had coins struck attributing to himself the godhead of Zeus. His effrontery was breathtaking; he scuttled the gods of his ancestors, including Adonis. He coveted above all the position of "top god" – hence "Epiphanes."

Daniel 11:40–45 The tone changes radically. We pass from a "prophecy after the occurrence" to a "prophecy of the end time." (See Dan. 10:40, "in the end time," and its linkage with Dan. 12:1 – a connection so close as to make regrettable the arbitrary separation of chapters.)

This is the assurance. Antiochus, for all his unexampled fury against the faithful and his absurd pride of place, will fall. The outcome is certain: in the large drama of time and ambition and the crooked lines of history, he has served his usefulness, which exceeded immeasurably his ambition. This was his function, according to the apocalypse granted Daniel; the tyrant sat enthroned, only to reveal the will of God with regard to the martyrs. In this he was no monarch at all, but a slave, in the image of those he enslaved. Sin also served, and the imperial sinner. He drew up the waters of grace from God's deep well.

To the faithful – to Daniel – the death of this monstrous ruler is uninteresting. Simply, he joined his wicked ancestors in Sheol. As for the faithful who became his victims, they were assured beforehand of the fate of the tyrant. Pondering their scriptures, they too were joined to a unanimous chorus of judgment.

If the history of the tyrant is recalled in a tone of fearsome condemnation, it is to remind the faithful of something ironic, a truth crucial as well to right understanding. Our (and their) instructors are not only the saints, companions in the fray, but the persecutors as well. How so? When submission to the divine will is refused, fire and sword descend. The law of retribution strikes up against the law of empire.

Does the unassuaged appetite of an Antiochus require martyrs, even as the forging of a sword requires a furnace? It must be so. And yet, and yet. An irony, all but unbearable, shows its face. Purified of all but bleak necessity, the freedom of the faithful grows perfect.

> I have often been threatened with death. I have to say, as a Christian that I don't believe in death without resurrection. If they kill me, I will rise again in the Salvadoran people. I tell you this without any boasting, with the greatest humility. As pastor, I am obliged by Divine command to give my life for those I love, who are all Salvadorans. Even for those who are going to assassinate me. If the threats are carried out, even now I offer my blood to God for the redemption and resurrection of El Salvador. Martyrdom is a grace of God I don't deserve. But if God accepts the sacrifice of my life, may my blood be the seed of liberty and the sign that hope may soon become reality. You may say, if they come and kill me, that I forgive those who did it. Hopefully they may realize that they will be wasting their time. A bishop will die, but the church of God, which is the people, will never perish.*
>
> *Oscar Romero*

*Salvadorean Archbishop Romero spoke these words on March 10, 1980. Fourteen days later he was killed by an assassin's bullet while saying Mass in a hospital chapel.

> If it should happen one day...that I become a victim of the terrorism which now seems ready to encompass all the foreigners living in Algeria, I would like my community, my church, my family, to remember than my life was given to God and to this country...I ask them to be able to associate such a death with the many other deaths which were just as violent, but forgotten through indifference and anonymity.
>
> I have lived long enough to know that I share in the evil which seems alas, to prevail in the world – even in that evil which would strike me blindly. I should like, when that times comes, to have a clear space which would allow me to beg forgiveness of God and of all my fellow human beings, and at the same time to forgive with all my heart the one who would strike me down. I could not desire such a death. It seems important to state this. I do not see in fact how I could rejoice, if this people I love were to be accused indiscriminately of my murder...
>
> And you also, the friend of my final moment, who would not be aware of what you were doing – Yes, for you also I wish this "thank you" and this *adieu,* and commend you to the God whose face I see in yours. And may we find each other, happy "good thieves," in paradise, if it please God, the Father of us both. Amen.*
>
> *Christian de Chergé*

A sign is raised over the royal catafalque; something of great moment is to occur. The time of bloody necessity is over. The people are liberated; the community breathes free.

Daniel 12:1 The Event *par excellence* is to take place "in those days," a phrase duly consecrated, announcing a flash point in time, an intervention. It is variously referred to as *kairos* – a moment of crisis, of divine irruption, an end time.

*De Chergé, the Cistercian abbot of Tibherine Monastery, near Algiers, was kidnapped and murdered by Muslim radicals in May, 1996, with six fellow monks. He wrote the letter excerpted above in 1994 and instructed his family to open it only after his death.

"In those days." The remarkable phrase is thrice repeated. We are not to miss the point.

On the Threshold of Tomorrow

Look, new sprouts push through the fields.
But which are thorns and which wheat
I do not know. Perhaps to the appetite
that is sated, all is chaff,
while to the hungry all is wheat.

Undistinguishable sounds, blows, footfalls
thud in the distance, an agonizing attack,
where the oppressed plant red
flames with their blood.
And the rains sweat and expand
into floods that shake the walls
of the oldest dams.

Lord, now is the time to send
your wisdom and kindness
to the tortured who, although
they have forgotten, need you as they hurl
themselves closer to the precipice.

Oh God, who trims the wick of the mind
and pours the oil of life, do not let
your lamps be overturned.
Let them illumine paths to your truth.

Plant love in the eyes of today's
and tomorrow's mighty. Do not let
their hearts close.

And do not let the hearts of the child
and the aged be strangers
to tenderness and hope.

Let the struggle of our time be short.
Let it be settled with justice.

Let the fortress of egos,
that huge barricade,
crumble. And let every treasure
go to every man. Let every garden
gate be open. But let no flower be crushed.
No single branch fall.

Vahan Tekeyan

The End Is Not Yet, But Nears

The Book of Daniel

12 "At that time Michael, the great prince, the protector of your people, shall arise. There shall be a time of anguish, such as has never occurred since nations first came into existence. But at that time your people shall be delivered, everyone who is found written in the book. 2Many of those who sleep in the dust of the earth shall awake, some to everlasting life, and some to shame and everlasting contempt. 3Those who are wise shall shine like the brightness of the sky, and those who lead many to righteousness, like the stars forever and ever. 4But you, Daniel, keep the words secret and the book sealed until the time of the end. Many shall be running back and forth, and evil shall increase."

5Then I, Daniel, looked, and two others appeared, one standing on this bank of the stream and one on the other. 6One of them said to the man clothed in linen, who was upstream, "How long shall it be until the end of these wonders?" 7The man clothed in linen, who was upstream, raised his right hand and his left hand toward heaven. And I heard him swear by the one who lives forever that it would be for a time, two times, and half a time, and that when the shattering of the power of the holy people comes to an end, all these things would be accomplished. 8I heard but could not understand; so I said, "My lord, what shall be the outcome of these things?" 9He said, "Go your way, Daniel, for the words are to remain secret and sealed until the time of the end. 10Many shall be purified, cleansed, and refined, but the wicked shall continue to act wickedly. None of the wicked shall understand, but those who are wise shall understand. 11From the time that the regular burnt offering is taken away and the abomination that desolates is set up, there shall be one thousand two hundred ninety days. 12Happy are those who persevere and attain the thousand three hundred thirty-five days. 13But you, go your way, and rest; you shall rise for your reward at the end of the days."

The End Is Not Yet, But Nears

Daniel 12 Let us concede it. These latter episodes of our book lack entirely the folkloric charm of the first chapters. Indeed, even if we approach them inquisitively, carefully, and concentratedly, so as to milk as much meaning as possible from them, they strike us as fragmented, abstract, unhinged.

What has happened to Daniel? There are, alas, no more stories about a superhuman Daniel and his miraculous pluckings from death. No more of this. Now he seems drawn into the irrational psyche of the kings; he walks in a house of mirrors, farther and farther, less and less our companion on the way. He dreams within dreams. And we scarce can follow.

As though this were not enough, it seems that in his waking hours, he walks another world than ours, among other companions than us humans. We cannot dwell there; we have no ticket of entrance.

He seems to have died, or (to keep the image of the scroll) to have crossed that stream whose bridge is upheld by angelic piers. He has crossed over.

And we? We have not died yet. So we lose him, this Lazarus, this revenant who comes and goes among angels and that astonishing, veiled Human One – and who seems more at home with them than with us!

It comes to this, one thinks. We shall have to bear with him as, let us not forget, he bears with us. He bears with us – incomplete humans, far short of twice born; we who are cursed or blessed, or both, with making do in a world of Make Do. *Ac si non esset Deus* – "as though God did not exist. Thus our world and the worldly powers make mock of

God, that Non-intervenor, that Referee standing twilit, obscure, in some neutral corner of the universe. Silent as the dead.

Perhaps this is a clue. In these chapters, we are told in effect that Daniel has seen God, the Human One. And has lived to tell of it. Language falls short; his hands drop to his sides. He tells it badly, haltingly, in fragments, bits and pieces – which is, of course, the only way such a Passover, so perilous and unprecedented a crossing of time's river, could be told. So to our story, concerning angels and one poor (and yet how dazzlingly rich) mortal, so like us, so unlike.

Daniel 12:1 Michael, "the great prince, the protector of your people," shall appear, and "everyone whose name is found written in the book shall be delivered." The scroll is elsewhere referred to as "a book of remembrance," containing names of "those who feared the Lord and thought of God's name" (Mal. 3:16). Such a book, its account kept by God, is an image common to Exodus, Psalms, Isaiah, Ezekiel, and Revelation, where it is referred to as "the book of life."

Daniel 12:2 This verse is seminal, extraordinary. Some would take it as the first reference in Hebrew scripture to the resurrection of the body (following Isa. 26:19). To others (following Ezek. 11:14–15) the text is far less spectacular. According to them the words indicate no more than the "second spring" of an Israel restored – which is to say, ancient themes revisited: the return from exile and the renewal of a people.

I lean toward Isaiah and to Daniel's leaning toward him. Expressions such as "those who sleep in the dust of the earth," and its near equivalent in Isaiah, "O dwellers in the dust, awake," are sufficiently striking. More, "the dust," referring either to the grave or to Sheol, is found in Isaiah, Job, and Ecclesiastes.

In any case, an immemorial trek of the spirit led to this verse, if one considers – even briefly – the strong implication in earlier scripture that no being survives beyond the grave: "Better a live dog than a dead lion" (Eccles. 9:4). More, a human afterlife, whatever that many mean, differs no whit from that of beasts (Eccles. 3:19). No great consolation here! Sheol is beyond God's outreach (Ps. 6:5; 88:4–2); yet early on, ca. 750 BCE, we encounter in Amos a radically new direction: now Sheol, too, is included in God's providence (Amos 9:2). As for the grave, it exerts no ultimate claim. Still, the earlier texts remain a kind of shadowy Sheol of the mind; there is as yet no trace of belief in resurrection. Then this.

Daniel 12:3 Regarding the *Maskillim,* or those "skilled in justice," or those "who have brought others to justice" – we have encountered these before: the faithful who persevere in spite of the tyrants, who observe torah and endure the cost. And who beckon others to a like fidelity. Quite literally, the lives and deaths of these "masters of justice" have rendered them apt for resurrection. Passionate for life, they turn inevitable realities on their head. They reverse the harsh law of the "realm of necessity," the "law of death" invoked in Genesis 3 and summoned again in Paul's letter to the Romans (Rom. 5:12).

Also we note the strong link with Isaiah 53:11. The "fourth servant song" identifies and praises, in the name of Jahweh, the same quality – the wisdom that brings others to justice. "By his knowledge shall my servant, the righteous one, bring many to be accounted righteous."

We have in such praise of the *Maskillim* an element both of division and of a deeper unity. They are summoned to unmask the injustices so often concealed under incantations of law and order. Thus unmasking the truth of things, they prepare people and institutions to accept their true vocation – service rather than ravenous self interest. Many, of course, would prefer that unsavory matters not be brought to light. Therefore the just must be prepared to pay up, and prepare others to do likewise.

Daniel 12:2–3 These verses must be accounted central to the faith of Christians as well as Jews. Matthew quotes to the letter (Matt. 13:43) the praise of the just and their consequent glory, merited in blood and tears.

Daniel 12:4 Now Daniel is urged to "seal up the vision" (as in Rev. 10:4). But in Revelation, a counter. The Lamb unseals one by one the seven seals of the mysterious scroll of history (Rev. 1:1 ff.). And later, John the Divine is told by a voice from heaven, "Seal up what the seven thunders have spoken!" (Rev. 10:4)

How comes this? Here we are, and here the multitudes of all the centuries since Daniel. And the book is in our hands, then is handed on, generation upon generation, legible and loved, that "sealed" book! It is open, and more. It is read and pondered and believed – and died for.

As a matter of fact (and more, a matter of faith, as would be insisted by many), the book is unsealed in every generation. It beckons us, this book. It would make saints of us, we the unlikeliest of candidates. Its angels haunt our days, its perils, pits and furnaces, the foolishness of king-knaves, the bravery of a few, the slavishness of multitudes – the images spill from the pages precipitously, into the mind, into motive and action.

Sealed? If so, ever so lightly sealed, and the seal easily broken, the scroll open to all – multitudes reading, pondering, learning, lingering over the book! Are we, then, who unseal the book to be accounted disobedient in so grave a matter? Believers or would-be believers – and yet disobedient?

Unsealed, or sealed? Let us put the matter this way: the book, in many images rejected or misapprehended, in many cultural enticements, in a multitude of lives, in shady motives and renegings, in yieldings to greed and lust and violence, in the call to read and respond and enact – in these and like refusals, the book remains sealed. Consult, in this matter of the sealed book, the experts. The honest among them (not all are honest) confess to considerable confusion around the seeming contradictions and lacunae. Why, for example, is Daniel absent from the testing in the furnace? What meaning is to be attached to the tortured imagery of the final chapters? And what of the identity, as well as the instruction, of "the one who looked like a man," the Human One? What to make of that mysterious "year, two years and half a year" of tribulation, borrowed also by Revelation? (Rev. 12:14) And so on, and so on.

At the least, let us venture this. The instructions concerning the revelation given Daniel contain a hint of invitation. That he (and we) rest content in obscure words and images, in the koans, the testing of heart and mettle. The puzzles stop the mind in its tracks; at the same time, they beckon us into the darkness of a deeper understanding.

Rhythms of rest are urged together with rhythms of search; each appointed to Daniel, to ourselves. Be not anxious or afraid. In due time light will be granted. Meantime do not be enslaved to darkness. Lift your eyes from the text; ponder the events of your lifetime, the signs of the times. Return again to the text. You will know.

And a caveat too. Not every "resting in the mystery" is to be judged courageous and wise. Nor is the search for light, though it purport to be of the Spirit, necessarily so. "There will come false prophets, who will deceive many" (Matt. 24:5).

No wonder the words of the angel set Daniel trembling, for the "time unsurpassed in distress since nations began…" And amid "the nations" and their crimes stands the "sign" of his own life, now resting in the spirit, now scaldingly in search of light. He falls to ground; again he rises and walks, intrepid and alone, deeper into a cave of darkness. A cave of ancestors. A place where Jeremiah speaks. Daniel will go on. And may that sign of his, the sign of a peerlessly faithful life, lead us aright in our appalling world, the hour's need, the chancy moment, the truth in jeopardy!

Meantime, despite its being sealed, the scripture is at hand; available, an anointing for the healing, the sanity we name faith. Daniel and his like, giants and heroes of the ages, are after all at our beck and call.

The story of Jesus stands open as well; we have only to *tolle et lege.** Those portions of the Word which are to remain sealed are in the main revelations regarding the future. And that future would seem, if a living faith is our quest, to be no small affair of ours.

* *Tolle et lege* – "Take, read!" According to St. Augustine's *Confessions,* these words, sung by a child from behind a courtyard wall, struck the saint as a divine imperative to take up the Bible and read what was written there. The result was his conversion.

Still, a further perplexity arises. Is not the instruction to seal the vision violated in the act of writing it down? Or did there once exist lines between the lines, portions of the vision since deleted or omitted, lying out of sight and mind, in that marvelous Dead Sea metaphor of sealed stone jars?

Suppose we take another tack. This: Daniel (or his later redactor, it makes no difference) is responsible for recounting the vision. Someone sets it down. There it blazes in our text. Pondering it, we are assured, will lend us vitality and coherence – as it will generations yet unborn. Which is to say, until the vision passes into belief and conduct, the word of God remains sealed. Thus the command to seal up the vision can be understood as an irony. Be blind as to whatever vision or visionary. Seal up the vision, forbid it, ignore it. As for the visionary, the law will deal with him!

The command even invites a deconstruction, one on a par with the announcement of Jahweh to Isaiah and Jeremiah. These, Jahweh announced, were appointed to speak the truth in season and out. And yet – speak, shout, mime, rage, endure as they would (the outcome was dourly predicted) – their effect on the people was nil. They faced their people unflinching, yet no one, not one of their own, would pay heed.

Jesus echoes the same hard estimate of truth telling and its effect. Through the blind incapacity of his auditors, the Word will be rendered null and void.

And yet, always a "yet." Though hedged about with darkness, the centuries since the prophets spoke can hardly be named dead. Against dire predictions, against all odds, the teachings of Isaiah, Jeremiah and Jesus are available and in our hands. Contrary to all dark foreboding, something went aright. Some ray of light and hope prevailed. Someone, some few, kept the scrolls unsealed, the script faithfully transmitted, the instructions taken seriously. Heroes and martyrs read, and ran to their death. Others of commoner stock (ourselves) discover in those pages sound reason to hope; to live in ways, unheroic though we be, that now and again confound a culture of death. The predictions of Jahweh and Jesus, dare we say, were proved in error? All to the good.

Of what value the harsh prophecies, then, portraying us humans as little more than a *massa damnata?* Were these no more than hyperbole, negatives heaped high by the Reader of hearts? A warning, in effect? A finger pointing to our inner darkness, our unacknowledged need, our capricious appetites, our disconcerting itch for violence, our pride of place – a litany of inhibitions piled high in the heart, forbidding the truth entrance?

Daniel was not made of light. We are not made of light. We are an admixture, weird and stormy and blind, of light and darkness, high noon and blear midnight. Our complicity with the world hardly renders us apt for the truth. But for the grace of God (the "unsealing" grace), we stand apt for the culture, and thereby damned. We see and refuse to see. And now and again – too rarely, God knows – we see and cry aloud. The truth, reality!

As to Daniel, his visions, instructions, parables, the example above all of that "man of desires," that survivor of tyrants and their machinations – all these riches rest on the page, before our eyes. Legible, yet hidden.

Let us imagine a circumstance. The gaze that falls on the holy pages is indifferent, bored – or openly hostile. It is the gaze of a tyrant, or of his sycophants, or of oppressors of the poor, the gaze of a "first family," of war makers, warriors, tycoons. Let us be for the moment – unreal. Generations of these come and go like shadows on a rock. They and we are trapped in a downward spiral of hopelessness. Let us surmise that for centuries no saint has been born, no martyr, no liberator. That the text knows only enemies of the text. In such a scenario the book remains unopened, twice sealed, laid underground in a stone jar, deep in a cave. Which is to say, buried in the darkness of the morally comatose.

In this scenario, which proceeds in our own day, principalities of the dark quality of Nebuchadnezzar or Belshazzar or Darius or Antiochus proceed unimpeded on their awful way. And what of us Christians? We offer no resistance but instead light-mindedly join the imperial adventurings, at least by silence, at most by a kind of moral assimilation. In this sense too scripture can be described as sealed.

And Daniel has all unwitting obeyed the instruction: seal up the vision. Given the world and its potentates, given the Fall, given ourselves – the Word of God cannot not be sealed up, thrice sealed, hidden, feared, detested, forgotten. Daniel and his like have set down a Word so consistent with their example, so unequivocal, stark, unyielding, that it has struck up against "the many," the *Harrabim,* the woefully blind. The word, the vision is stuck there on stuttering tongues.

In this sense, the story of Jesus too is sealed. Let a crisis arise, a "time of tribulation." A war. And the plain sense of his teaching – together with his exemplary life and death – will be declared in one way or another out of touch, irrelevant, not to be taken literally. The Word will yet again be judged and found wanting; it will be deemed a personal rather than a social or political instruction, *passé* or idealistic or useful only as reference point to the end time.

The Sermon on the Mount will be superseded by a pagan casuistry, perennially useful to war makers, perennially beside the Christian point. In such times scripture becomes the tomb of Christ. The living way degenerates into a philosophic *tour de force* in the shadow of which Christians hide out, pondering consensually the way of the world. Lost there, in a Dantesque thicket.

Daniel 12:5 ff. An epilogue, a majestic scene – indeed, a judgment. Heavenly beings intervene; one "clothed in linen" (see Dan. 10:5), "standing above the waters of the stream." This majestic one raises both arms to heaven (Dan. 12:7). Then appear two "witnesses" to the oath, as required (Deut. 19:15). The oath is thus sustained. The angelic witnesses adhere closely to biblical law as they testify to the crimes of Antiochus against God's people. The geography is wondrously specific. To Daniel it would seem eternity is hardly a strange land; its spirits enter time and this world, and both remain intact. (A sign, so to be taken? A momentary glimpse, no sooner granted than gone, of an Incarnation to come?)

The heavenly witnesses span the stream, a living bridge between heaven and earth. Creation groans, draws a deep breath. The angels prepare for judgment. It is as though the river (of time, of empire) passed between them. They are firmly planted there, piers of the bridge; the river flows beneath. Thus time moves and moves, bearing all before. Bearing all except the witnesses, those piers, upholding, guarding, allowing passage. God's word abides; the two stand there, steadfast "one this side, one the other of the stream." Then the oath is pronounced in a setting of liturgical grandeur and solemnity.

Daniel 12:6 It would seem that the translation of the Revised Standard Version, "wonders," violates the sense here. "Wonders" would refer to the visions themselves, not to the horrible events that made such epiphanies necessary, even (though charged with fear) welcome. "Fearful destruction" (as in Dan. 8:24) seems closer to the sense.

Daniel's vocation meantime is unchanged; his life remains brutally appointed. He is a mode of God' presence; he is to endure the time of the tyrant. This for the sake of his people, as always. The implication is plain: to whom else can the lorn tribe look for strength and direction? They take breath, take heart from him to go on. He resuscitates their failing spirit; his courage is a contagion; if he can survive, so can they. He has never once separated the Word from the way. The two are one. Walk, then, at my side!

Given the predatory nature of imperial wrath, the visions can be said to offer a chilly comfort. God's hope for the world, though delayed, put upon, derided, frustrated, brutally crushed, the martyrs disposed of, the prophets gagged will nonetheless *not* be finally frustrated. Is this not enough, this sorry, last-ditch virtue we call hope?

"How long, this time of suffering?" The question reverberates through scripture. Here, notably, the question is raised by one of the angelic visitants, those deep-founded, steady piers of the bridge. And the visitant questions not his companion but the "man in white linen, who stood upstream." Is this latter a vessel of superior wisdom. Does he stand nearer the source, the watershed of time, of the river? Does he hearken there to the voice of the headwaters?

It is an angel, existing outside time and tribulation, who raises the crucial question – a question which to our way of thinking (and hoping and suffering) would sit better on the lips of Daniel. What has this otherworldly being, an angel, to do with the muck of our luckless world?

Still, the angel stands at the river, in time, visible to human eyes. This peerless spirit who questions: it is as though he stood surrogate for questioning Daniel. The angel stands in the river of time. Is this, perhaps, a gift to us – not an angelic immunity from the common suffering, but acceptance, immersion in the human lot? And through the immersion of such watchful love – immersion in time and this world – do not our tormented questionings become his own? Are such holy beings not named and revered as guardian angels? And being appointed to guard and cherish, heal and guide, must it not follow that they taste something of the bitter lees of human life?

Another implication, also from an angel. "How long?" implies that it has already been too long, that too many have perished. And what, pray, might God proffer by way of relief? If there is no relief, or so little as hardly to deflect the killing blade – if there is no intervention, no justifying, no judgment against high crime – then why?

And when the river turns to blood, and seems bottomless and wide as a covering deluge, who then can tread the waters? What angel will serve to bridge them?

The questions are unutterably deep, though they beckon the inquiring mind. Who is this God, this non-intervenor, this Man Clothed in Linen, who stands upstream? Is he there; is he not there; is he a mirage? And if indeed he stands there, why is he silent; why does he not call halt to the murderous centuries and their supernumeraries?

Wait. At distance an angel stands there too, at the stream of time – amid rapacious waters which we thought too deep, too strong – prevailing, a current sweeping all before.

It is the faithful ones, whether angelic or human, who stand face to face with the Mystery, who make the impassioned appeal. Angels, *fides quaerens intellectum?* – their faith in search of understanding?

An angel is our instructor. And we learn that the raising of such questions is crucial to faith itself. Let us hear it, learn it by rote. The questioning of God regarding the suffering of the innocent lies at the heart of faith – which is to say, at the heart of the human.

Let us linger over it, the scene before us; it offers a strange consolation. God is questioned; the seeker is mysterious, an invisible one presumably free of the bonds of our time and place. For the moment, the same being is palpable, visible, audible. Are we to know that the angels standing at either bank of the river are closer to our condition that we dare imagine? Their presence, their questionings – these say "yes."

They interrogate the Man in White. Thus they bless us, despite our confusion. Raise the questions, they imply; raise them loud and clear; raise them in groanings of spirit, in private and before others. Raise them in worship; let your anguish, your passion for justice, your sense of violation at the omnipresence of injustice – let these be published far and wide! Shall faith permit of no perplexities? The angels deny it, urging perplexities of their own.

Another tack. Are we mortals to be accounted dullards, or is our Instructor so forbidding (or so uncertain, of so little command) that we must sit in place and, like children in a school for drudges, must keep a silent tongue or risk the ferrule? The angels say "no." Are we in dire times to become numbed victims; to take, whether in stride or in stumbling the cruel course of the world, its bludgeonings and spleen – and say nothing, question nothing? The angels forbid such a course.

Thus our scripture. Its images of river and holy bridge builders offer not a response, but something else: something, one dares say, that is better. They offer approval of the questions. And of the questioners. Such questions, initiated by angels, hover on the air of ancient times and places – and our own. What riches are ours for the taking, bleak though the times! The Word of God, and its wealth of icons, builders of bridges, spirits withstanding and standing by! Heroes and saints, and now angels, each portrayed as a questioning servant of the Most High. Let us learn, and rejoice.

An impassioned hectoring of God is thus declared blessed, a sign of faithfulness. Here, humans and angels are in dialogue – and in what fervent contest! What a "night of now done dark" wrestling with the Word! And with the Speaker of that Word as well ("clothed in linen, standing upstream") – this dialogue and contest, both.

Dabhar, "the word," is translated as "a driving forward of that which is behind." We imagine the Speaker standing there, the word he speaks driving the listener forward. But where driven? To that place from which the Speaker has come? Or in the Christian sense (the midrash we make all but instinctively), to that place where the Speaker will go, the gospel place? Or yet another topography – to the place where the listener, in his own time, must go? "Go, Daniel," he said. And "Blessed is the one who has patience and perseveres."

As for our darkened understanding, our slow heartbeat, our twilit conscience, the mis-directions we avidly follow, the grace we refuse – these drive us backward into moral regression, where we choose to be – stuck, fragmented, distracted, governed by fear, and riddled with a darkness born of pride. Fallen. We balk, we must be driven forward. Must hear the Word.

Driven, forward. The term is hardly complimentary, implying as it does a resemblance to oxen or dray horses; burdened, in servitude, even subject now and again to a flogging. The word of God drives us forward, who are perennially, congenitally "behind." (No need of dwelling on that sorry circumstance: the Bible rubs our soul in it.)

Still, granted the sublime estate of the questioner, the heroism of Daniel, who stands listening, the setting and the urgency – despite all, one must concede that little or no enlightenment arrives downstream. We stand there like Daniel at the mighty keystone and crux of the matter.

Yet there is some solace, even if small: the evident approval of the question together with the non-answer. The comfort is icy, but it must nonetheless be taken to heart. We have in such episodes an evidence, a reassurance even. However opaque the response to our query, God has hearkened.

Are we to be resigned to this, and pass on to other matters? Let us say that today also, believers pose the bloodshot question. And lucky we, if we also have a surrogate, a champion, someone (or even two) to speak for us, "standing on either bank of the river." We know something, not much, of these two. Daniel perhaps knows more.

This he knows, and wonders at (and so do we) – the courtesy and attentiveness with which they read his heart, posing the difficulty which lies heavy and unspoken on him: "How long?" And then the response, but so opaque! The angel shakes his head – the first of the smiling angels, one ventures: "These words are to be kept secret and sealed until the end time."

Let us then suppose that Daniel the seeker bows out, declines to pursue the meaning of that strange time frame, "a year, two years, a half year." In his mind a conclusion is reached. It has a sound; the abrupt shutting of a door; or the final closing of a book. Thus: God is the Impenetrable One. The mystery of evil and the suffering of the innocent are a territory "upstream"; there the weather is befogged. And more: the terrain is off bounds, forbidden. One alone is entitled to walk there, to stand there.

We linger, one hopes not overlong, over this episode. It is so painful – a full measure of the pain of life itself. And yet, and yet. One factor is to be taken in account: the response of God (the non-response, hermetic, evasive as it seems) has shifted the status of the question. And, one thinks, deliberately. Something is implied; some light offered. An aspect Daniel had forgotten or neglected to probe is in some measure illumined. Perhaps in frustration or numbness of spirit, the point had not occurred to him. Perhaps he turned away from an implication that could spell further trouble.

There is a concurrence (though a different emphasis) in the answer offered the martyrs of Revelation 9–11, and the response to Daniel. In the former, the stress and angst of the question (time unrequited, justice delayed) are relieved somewhat. In this way: there is a "completion" to be attained of "the number of their fellow servants…to be killed as they had been." Which is to say, short of justice for all, there is simply no justice. And God knows it, takes it in account.

We have the famous "time, times, and half a time" (echoed in Dan. 7:25 and 8:14; also in Rev. 11:2; 12:14; 13:5). Hidden in this drumbeat of repetition is a reassurance of sorts. The time of travail is delimited, strictly contained. But still, the atrocious times roll on, interminably it seems, to our own hour. Evil, like a ravening dog, will have its day. Every day. All days.

So Daniel and his question (and the angel who speaks for him) are set down with a slight thump. With no more light than we children of equally dark times can claim.

"How long to the end?" Daniel is granted a non-response and is sent once more on his way (Dan. 12:9, 13). Not greatly enlightened – only slightly so. Not greatly strengthened – perplexity still aches in his bones. Unsatisfied, he tries once more. And is granted nothing more.

There is in effect no more to be said. It is simply implied that he has sufficient light to walk by. (And sufficient darkness, that he might tread the world with forethought and care.) In a strange, intermittent light-cum-darkness, timorous step by step, Daniel is to go – and go on. It is called faith. And in God's time he will be known the faithful one.

Daniel 12:9–10 Is the future, then, bound ineluctably to the past, like a captive to a stake? Are the wicked to push on unrepentant, and the holy ones immemorially to pay up? Only this: for a time, for a time only. This is the comfort, not far short of icy, offered by the apocalyptic word.

We can at least venture this summing-up. Evil perennially renewed, the wickedness and inhumanity of authorities and structures – in face of these, human explanations, taken of themselves, fail utterly. The problem is, to speak redundantly, that the "problem of evil" is not a problem at all; it is a mystery.

The world of the Fall, obsessed as it is with scientific measurements and measurable sciences, is not pleased with the word "mystery." The word smacks of charlatanry, obfuscation, god talk. Also (though this is seldom discussed, and is equally offensive to the makers and breakers), mystery implies limits, boundaries, even (horror!) – incapacities. The world's way of proceeding is a problem-solution equation, universally applied. Everything, even the knottiest knot, can be analyzed and fixed. Including, with the help of a psychiatric spelunker, those fast-knotted spirits who are impelled to run to some god or other for their "fix" on the world or themselves. Considered in this way, lacking access or possibility of intervention, wickedness and crime degenerate into a "problem." Things would go better (the clock again), people would become better, given education or legal abortion or the death penalty or fewer immigrants or one more (only one more – this one will "fix" things for good!) – war. By such misreading of reality, the worst intentions or the best add up to very little or no significant change. Which is to say, our plight.

The biblical implication is worlds apart from the above. Our age of technology and technique cannot in any serious way renew or pacify or humanize. "The world" thus understood is stuck; this is the biblical datum. Stuck not in space, but in its own assumptions. Once mystery is jettisoned, and we mortals left to our own resources, we enter a nightmare; the realm of a riddle proposed by a stone sphinx.

And for Christians, the "Mystery" Daniel pays tribute to includes the majestic transcendence of God, and God's access as well. We are told of One who stood before Daniel, transfixed. And of One who walked among us, welcoming, healing, reconciling. Even for sake of such as ourselves, O wonderful! In Christ the mystery of evil meets its match; one almost says (say it!) is surpassed by the mystery of goodness. The tyrant is overcome, even as he wreaks death on the martyr Christ. Thus the victim becomes a witness to (among other, more sublime truths) the failure of the destroyer to destroy. The dead Man walks abroad.

A Penitent Speaks

You come toward me
prestigious in your wounds,
those frail and speechless bones.
Your credentials –
dying somberly for others.
What a burden, gratitude, fake and true vows,
crucifixes
grislier than the event –
and then the glory gap –
larger than life
begetting less than life,
pieties that strike healthy eyes
blind;
Believe! Believe! Christians
tapping down a street
in harness to their seeing-eye god.
Only in solitude,
a passing tic of insight
gone as soon as granted
– I see You come toward me free,
free at last.
Can one befriend his God?
The question is inadmissable, I know.
Nonetheless a fiery recognition
lights us;
broken by life,
making our comeback.

D. B.

Long before the coming of Christ, an end is declared to the pretension and arrogance of an Antiochus. He would seize upon the end time, and in a show of domination claim it, declaring his realm as the final form of politics (mass murder, repression), and of religion (Zeus in the holy place). But: the power of the destroyer of the holy people is brought to an end. Will the tyrant take heed at last? Will he know his limits?

It bears repeating, since the matter goes to the heart of the biblical message: we humans cannot – however virtuous our striving, however noble our genius, however "progressive" our system of political amelioration or revolution – usher in the era of justice and peace known as the realm of God. Thus the plain sense of our scripture.

As for Daniel, an abrupt command is issued. It is thrice repeated. "Go on your way." Not any way at all: not a wayward, confused detour. Rather a way that, however obscure, is guided and girded about by angels. For again, the angels are guided by another, the Man Clothed in Linen.

Faith, it would seem, has this advantage – the believer concentrates mind and heart upon means that dovetail nicely with the end, the "end time," the "realm." Let the seeker, like Daniel, concentrate on such means as make that stupendous advent less unlikely, less distant. Let the seeker become a seer. Let him pursue the truth through means that accommodate, welcome, befit the truth. And the seer will come to understand that the Realm nears. This because the means, like a lowly, all but invisible seed lodged in good soil, in sign and portent and hope of harvest, contain the end itself.

Finally (Dan. 12:13), the promise is issued: "You will take your rest, and will stand in your allotted place at the end." The promise of resurrection envelops Daniel in a mantle of mercy. The harshest times have probed and purified him. And found him faithful. The outcome is assured.

Those who endure such times as Daniel's are invited to a similar hope, induced by a like assurance. Meantime they (and their angels) are free to probe the intent of God. As we have insisted, such questioning implies no serious doubt, only an intense trouble of mind. (A difference of note!) Such questions in fact do honor to the mind, in strenuous exercise of its native powers, asking again and again how divine goodness can be squared with the evil that daily assaults us.

Little wonder the questions that hang burning on the air. Small wonder too that within their own communities, such questioners are reproved, for indulging in the apocalyptic. Of course the times are out of joint! But why this brimstone mentality? And implied, though seldom stated the old reproach: One can do nothing…

Are we to conclude that these appalling things, "the destroyer of the holy people," "the horrible abomination…set up" – that such are to be met with indifference, with moral numbing?

Of note in our text: no praise is offered the indifferent or numb, the non-questioners among the faithful. But those whose anguished sense of justice churns in the gut have as credential and blessing the Book of Daniel.

The same book became a credential of Jesus (Mark 13) as the hour of his Passion neared. A resource and promise. And for ourselves, enduring as we must an age that is redundantly banal and brutal, the Book of Daniel speaks, with the tongues of angels and humans, of celebrating under travail. Come rack, come rope!

The Cure at Troy

Human beings suffer,
They torture one another,
They get hurt and get hard.
No poem or play or song
Can fully right a wrong
Inflicted and endured.

The innocent in jail
Beat on their bars together.
A hunger-striker's father
Stands in the graveyard dumb.
The police widow in veils
Faints at the funeral home.

History says, "Don't hope
On this side of the grave."
But then, once in a lifetime
The longed-for tidal wave
Of justice can rise up
And hope and history rhyme.

So hope for a great sea-change
On the far side of revenge.
Believe that a further shore
Is reachable from here.
Believe in miracles
And cures and healing wells.

Call miracle self-healing;
The utter self-revealing
Double take of feeling
If there's fire on the mountain
Or lightning and storm
And a god speaks from the sky –

That means someone is hearing
The outcry and the birth-cry
Of new life at its term.

Seamus Heaney

Looking at Stars

The God of curved space, the dry
God, is not going to help us, but the son
whose blood spattered
the hem of his mother's robe.

Jane Kenyon

The Author

Daniel Berrigan, S.J. lives in New York City, where he is a member of West Side Jesuit Community. An activist, public speaker, author of more than forty books, and part-time teacher at Fordham University, he holds workshops at conferences and retreats around the world.

Books by Daniel Berrigan

Prose

The Bride: Essays in the Church
The Bow in the Clouds
Consequences: Truth and Love, Love at the End
They Call Us Dead Men
Night Flight to Hanoi
No Bars to Manhood
The Dark Night of Resistance
America is Hard to Find
The Geography of Faith (with Robert Coles)
Absurd Convictions, Modest Hopes (with Lee Lockwood)
Jesus Christ
Lights on in the House of the Dead
The Raft Is Not the Shore (with Thich Nhat Hanh)
A Book of Parables
Uncommon Prayer: A Book of Psalms

Beside the Sea of Glass: The Song of the Lamb
The Words our Savior Taught Us
The Discipline of the Mountain
We Die Before We Live
Portraits: Of Those I Love
Ten Commandments for the Long Haul
The Nightmare of God
Steadfastness of the Saints
The Mission
To Live in Peace: Autobiography
A Berrigan Reader
Stations (with Margaret Parker)
Sorrow Built a Bridge
Whereon to Stand (Acts of Apostles)
Minor Prophets, Major Themes
Ezekiel: Vision in the Dust
Isaiah: Spirit of Courage, Gift of Tears

Poetry

Time Without Number
Encounters
The World for Wedding Ring
No One Walks Waters
False Gods, Real Men
Trial Poems (with Tom Lewis)
Prison Poems
Selected and New Poems
May All Creatures Live
Block Island
Jubilee
Tulips in the Prison Yard
Homage (to G.M. Hopkins)

Drama

The Trial of the Catonsville Nine

The Woodcuts

To illustrate key episodes of this challenging text, I employed an ancient method of printing: the wood block. First, after reading and re-reading both the biblical Book of Daniel, and my friend Daniel Berrigan's commentaries, I conceived drawings on paper, which I then traced in reverse onto wood. Then I cut away the areas that appear white in the illustrations and rolled the remaining wood surfaces with ink. Next, rice paper was burnished against the inked surface, and removed. The visual boldness of the final images results from the integration of each concept with its execution and with the printing process itself, a boldness that I hope inspires each reader as he or she meditates and grows with Daniel.

Robert F. McGovern

Other Titles from Plough

Discipleship

Living for Christ in the Daily Grind

J. Heinrich Arnold

A collection of thoughts on following Christ in the nitty-gritty of daily life. Includes sections on love, humility, forgiveness, leadership, community, suffering, salvation, and the kingdom of God.

$16.00 / £10.50

Salt and Light

Living the Sermon on the Mount

Eberhard Arnold

Talks and writings on the transformative power of a life lived by Jesus' revolutionary teachings in the Sermon on the Mount.

$15.00 / £10.00

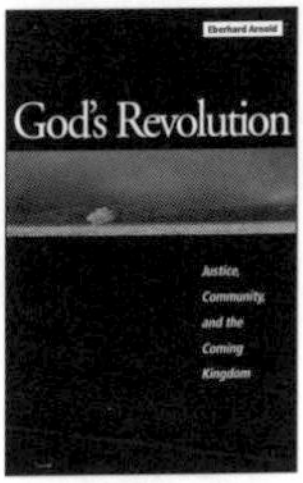

God's Revolution

Justice, Community, and the Coming Kingdom

Eberhard Arnold

Topically arranged excerpts from the author's talks and writings on the church, community, marriage and family issues, government, and world suffering.

$15.00 / £9.00

The Individual and World Need

Eberhard Arnold

One of Arnold's most compelling works, this essay explores the relationship of the individual to world sin and suffering and directs us clearly to a solution.

$4.00 / £3.00

The Gospel in Dostoyevsky

Edited by the Bruderhof

An introduction to the "great God-haunted Russian" comprised of passages from *The Brothers Karamazov*, *Crime and Punishment*, and *The Idiot.*

$15.00 / £10.00

The Violence of Love

Oscar Romero

Compiled and trans. by James R. Brockman, S.J.

In Romero's words we encounter a man of God humbly and confidently calling us to conversion and action. Those who let his message touch them will never see life in the same way again.

$14.00 / £9.50

Death Blossoms

Reflections from a Prisoner of Conscience

Mumia Abu-Jamal

This new collection of short vignettes and reflections examines the deeper dimensions of existence and testifies powerfully to the invincibility of the human spirit.

$12.00 / £8.00

The Plough

A Publication of the Bruderhof Communities

A quarterly journal with articles on issues and news items of interest to seekers for whom social justice and the call of the Gospel are one and the same.

$10.00 / year **£7.00 / year**

To order call **800-521-8011** (US) or **0800 269 048** (UK)

Also available from Plough

What transformed two priests into two "holy outlaws?"

Disarmed and Dangerous

The Radical Lives and Times of Daniel and Philip Berrigan

Murray Polner and Jim O'Grady

448 pp., hardcover
~~$30.00~~ **$21.00**
~~£21.00~~ **£15.00**

What made two traditional Catholics into the two most wanted men of J. Edgar Hoover's FBI? And how did they evolve from their pious, second-generation immigrant beginnings to become the most famous (some would say notorious) religious rebels of their day?

Disarmed and Dangerous, the first full-length biography of the Berrigan brothers, addresses these questions with an incisive and illuminating account of their rise to prominence as civil rights and antiwar activists. It also traces their careers as constant thorns in the side of an authoritarian church, as well as their leadership roles in the Plowshares movement – a highly controversial campaign of civil disobedience against the arms trade that isn't over yet.

To order call **800-521-8011** (US) or **0800 269 048** (UK)